NAUVOO RESTORED

*W*e can't stay in this [temple] but a little while.

We have got to build another house. It will be a larger house than this,

and a more glorious one. And we shall build a great many houses.

We shall come back here…and build houses all over

the continent of North America. [1]

—Brigham Young, January 2, 1846

NAUVOO RESTORED

Photography by Robert Casey

Written and Compiled by Margie McRae Brown

Designed by Sonja Jorgenson

The Living Scriptures®

Ogden, Utah

CONTENTS

PRODUCER'S NOTE

I desire this book to be a beautiful photographic memorial to the people, events, places

and restored buildings of Nauvoo; that it reflect the faith and testimony of those known

and unknown who accepted and lived the restored gospel—leaving us the powerful witness of their lives

in the "beautiful city" that they labored to establish in a hostile wilderness.

Jared F. Brown

Text copyright ©2002 Margie McRae Brown
Jacket and book design ©2002 Living Scriptures, Inc.
Photography by Robert Casey and ©2001, 2002 Living Scriptures, Inc. except where noted. All photographs of historic buildings, objects and portraiture courtesy of **Nauvoo Restoration, Inc.**, Nauvoo, Illinois unless otherwise noted. Temple photographs courtesy of The Church of Jesus Christ of Latter-day Saints, Nauvoo Temple Project, unless otherwise noted. All historical images reproduced with permission from respective owners.

Published by The Living Scriptures®
Ogden, Utah

The production team gratefully acknowledges the contribution of the following people and organizations to the success of this book: The Church of Jesus Christ of Latter-day Saints Nauvoo Temple Project, including Elder Ron Prince; Carol Hill and the staff at Nauvoo Restoration, Inc.; Community of Christ, World Headquarters, Independence, Missouri including Susan Naylor and Joyce Shireman, Joseph Smith Historic Center; Nauvoo State Park; Laurie Bonnell Stephens and staff of Trek West, Inc., including Sherry Bonnell Wade, Margie Nauta Lee, Katilyn Haun, Linda Cottle, Nancy Belliston, Heidi Barlow and Dan Thomas; Cathren L. Warner; Bill Slaughter and staff at Church Archives, The Church of Jesus Christ of Latter-day Saints, Salt Lake City, Utah; Union Station John M. Browning Firearms Museum, Ogden, Utah; International Society, Daughters of the Utah Pioneers; Museum of Church History and Art, including Ron Read; Dan Emerson, Pinnacle Marketing, Ogden, Utah; Latter-day Harvest, Inc., including Randall Varney, Corey and Amber Jensen; Jerry and Betti McLeod; Chris and Ian Frogley; C. Michael Trapp; and the many dedicated people from Nauvoo and other cities in Illinois, Iowa, Missouri and Utah who worked as models, assistants and wranglers to recreate the stirring emotion of the events of Nauvoo, 1839–46.

The production team: Jared F. Brown, executive producer; Bryan Jensen, creative director; Sonja Jorgenson, art director and senior designer; Margie McRae Brown, author; Robert Casey, photographer; Eric Fenton, production designer; Melanie Ruth Lee, on-site wardrobe and makeup supervisor; Krisee Casey and Eric Hasek, photo assistants; Valerie Holladay and Kim Wood, editors; Sherry Stephens, indexing.

First Printing, 2002
Printed in China by Palace Press, International
10 9 8 7 6 5 4 3 2 1

ISBN 1-56473-178-2

PREVIOUS PAGE: A view of the Seventies Hall

PHOTOGRAPHER'S NOTE

On our last day of shooting, we worked with a young man named David, who shared an important thought. At the end of Parley Street, the pioneers had to make a decision: either move forward, somehow crossing the vast river, or turn back. Those who chose to cross the Mississippi went on to achieve great things.

Sooner or later, we all come to the end of a Parley Street and have to make choices. This came for me on the day of September 11, 2001. Our flight to Nauvoo was cancelled. No car rentals were available; there were no flights until further notice.

ABOVE: Robert Casey with Dwight Handyside, depicting the great Fox/Sac orator and diplomat, Chief Keokuk, with his staff of authority and peace pipe. Photo by Krisee Casey.

I hopped into my little red Jetta and began an incredible journey to Nauvoo. The first night on the road I slept in the front seat of my car—a very minor inconvenience. It took me two and a half days to reach Nauvoo.

I have thought many times since of my forefathers leaving their homes, knowing they would never see those homes or their beautiful temple again. Learning of their daily hardships of travel, lack of comforts and daily endurance have made this a humbling and beautiful experience for me. It has given me greater insight to the lives of those who once walked, worked, laughed and cried on these very same streets.

In order to accurately reflect the spirit of the journal entries within this book, we needed the right conditions. I have no question in my mind that the prayers of many were answered each time we traveled to photograph Nauvoo.

My thanks to Bryan Jensen, Sonja Jorgenson and Eric Fenton, the LSI Design team; our "Finder of All Things," Jerry McLeod, and his wife, Betti; my two photo assistants, Eric Hasek and my daughter, Krisee; and Melanie Lee, who did the styling and costuming. My gratitude for friends at Pictureline

ABOVE: One of the photographer's favorite photographs: Yancee Bell portrays Sarah Granger Kimball.

in Salt Lake City; Cory Waite of Royce Photo; and Jerry Nelson. Carol Hill of NRI and Joyce Shireman of Community of Christ were also so kind and helpful in providing access to Nauvoo's historical sites.

A very special thanks to Jared and Margie Brown for creating and supporting this project. And last, I am grateful for a mother, unfortunately now departed, who taught me what to do at the end of Parley Street. This is for her.

Robert M. Casey

AUTHOR'S NOTE

The people who built Nauvoo are God's precious jewels to me. Nauvoo is an inspiration. Studying Nauvoo will swell your heart, moisten your eyes, and enlarge your understanding of the greatest of gospel principles while clarifying dates and perspective of Church history. The depth of this beautiful photographic work grew as I studied.

Nauvoo was an amazing time, place and people. The Prophet Joseph was a pattern of Christ. He wanted to give everyone all God gave him. He gave us all that was wisdom to give, then pleaded with us to use the gift of the Holy Ghost to receive more.

Joseph was loving, generous, fun, and patient. His friends were the best; his enemies, the worst.

Hyrum, John Taylor and Willard Richards were loyal to the end: forever witnesses of the martyrdom and the truth of the Restoration of the gospel of Jesus.

Five of Joseph's apostles became Church Presidents. Studying their lives, personalities and teachings creates joy. They were men filled with obedience to the principle of charity.

The Saints were also obedient; and although, at times, the "natural man" got the better of them, most stayed the course. They reported many miracles, including the transfiguration of Brigham Young to Joseph's voice and manner. The accounts of this fascinating event were numerous and indisputable. Four of my own ancestors separately reported it with no discrepancies. Hundreds recorded it in journals. It is a documented fact.

I wanted my name to appear on this book as Margie Ashby Stringham Mackay Murphy McRae Brown to honor my five sets of great-grandparents who established families and homes, and received temple blessings in Nauvoo. I love and revere them.

Sonja Jorgenson and Robert Casey did their work perfectly. They were ready to board a plane to Nauvoo on September 11, 2001. I express my thanks to Robert, who drove his car to Nauvoo to

photograph during the summer before the leaves turned. Sonja contacted all models and officials to schedule the photography. She also trimmed my exuberantly abundant copy to become this wonderful book.

LEFT: *Margie Brown leans against the wall of the Webb Blacksmith Shop in Nauvoo.* ABOVE: *A depiction of Eunice McRae, a great-great-grandmother of the author, hiding a small barrel of gun powder.* RIGHT: *A depiction of Mary Ann Young, wife of Brigham Young, and daughter Vilate, carrying apples behind the Brigham Young Home.*

I am grateful for the many good books, journals and scholarly works on Nauvoo. Mike Trapp, a master historian and resident of Nauvoo, shared his knowledge freely. Thanks and love to all who worked with me including Jared, Jarilynne, Daniel, Mark, Michelle, Matt, Danelle, Christine, Rachel, Karl, and Coral.

Margie Brown

INTRODUCTION

*B*eginning in 1839, a group of destitute and emotionally exhausted families gathered under the leadership of their prophet, Joseph Smith. They sought to escape persecution in Missouri as they settled on a horseshoe bend of the Mississippi and accepted the challenges of a malarial swampland. Originally called Commerce, Illinois, the name of the city was changed by Joseph to an eloquent Hebrew name, *Nauvoo*, meaning *peaceable*, *fruitful* and *beautiful*. Here they planted crops, trees, vineyards and flowers. They harvested and built substantial homes, businesses and a magnificent quarried limestone temple to their God. In only seven years, this noble and remarkable people, from elderly to infant, built a metropolitan area of 20,000, one of the larger cities in the United States. Their voices speak to us in this story of faith and sacrifice, told by their own hand, through inspiring journal entries and historical records.

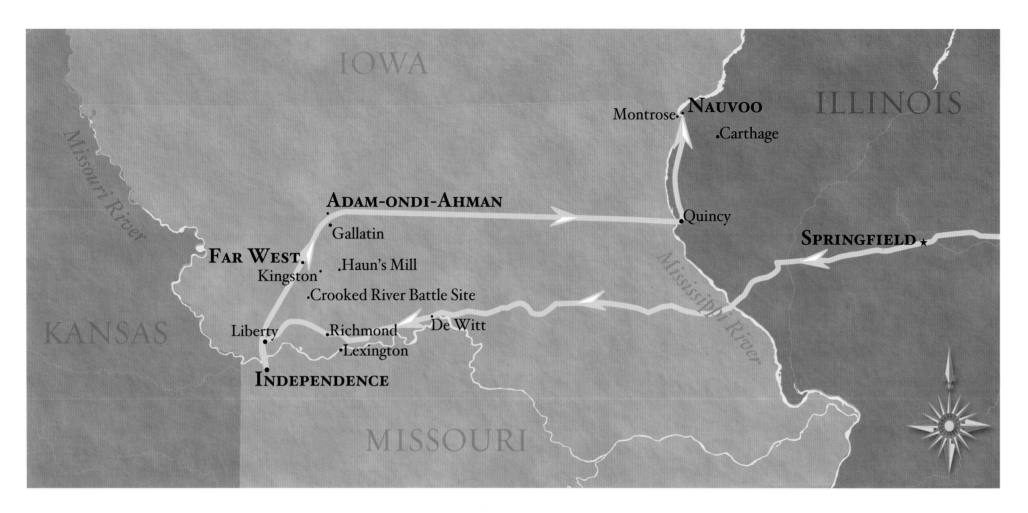

CHRONOLOGY OF IMPORTANT NAUVOO EVENTS

26 Jan. 1839   Committee on Removal [from Missouri] organized by Brigham Young

Feb. 1839   Large-scale migration from Missouri began

22 Apr. 1839   Joseph Smith arrived in Quincy after several months imprisonment in Missouri

30 Apr. 1839   Joseph Smith negotiated land purchases in Iowa and Illinois

22 July 1839   A "day of God's power" manifested as many were healed in Nauvoo and Montrose

16 Dec. 1839   The Nauvoo Charter signed in Springfield, Ill.

15 Aug. 1840   Doctrine of baptism for dead taught at funeral

15 Jan. 1841   First Presidency issued a proclamation urging all Saints "scattered abroad" to gather to Nauvoo

6 Apr. 1841   Cornerstones of Nauvoo Temple laid

8 Nov. 1841   Nauvoo Temple baptismal font was dedicated

17 Mar. 1842   Relief Society founded

Spr. 1842   Wentworth letter and Book of Abraham published in *Times and Seasons*

4 May 1842   Joseph Smith gave first endowments in upper room of Red Brick Store

16 May 1843   Revelation explaining the necessity of eternal marriage

12 July 1843   Revelation received concerning the New and Everlasting Covenant

Jan. 1844   Joseph Smith became candidate for president of United States

7 June 1844   Conspirators published the only edition of *Nauvoo Expositor*

10 June 1844   Nauvoo city council ordered destruction of of *Expositor*

18 June 1844   Joseph Smith placed Nauvoo under martial law

22 June 1844   Governor Ford insisted Joseph and Hyrum go to Carthage to answer charges against them

24 June 1844   Joseph and Hyrum went to Carthage

27 June 1844   Joseph and Hyrum murdered in Carthage by a mob

8 Aug. 1844   Brigham Young transfigured before the people and the Twelve sustained as the presiding quorum of the Church

Oct. 1845   Church leaders announced intention to move to the West

Oct. 1845   Saints prepared for exodus to the West

10 Dec. 1845   Endowment ordinance work began in Temple

4 Feb. 1846   First group crossed the Mississippi River

Mid-Feb. 1846   Brigham Young and others of the Twelve left Nauvoo

1–20 July 1846   Mormon Battalion recruited for U. S. war with Mexico

Sept. 1846   Battle of Nauvoo and evacuation of poor Saints

As spring bloomed with lively green grasses and abundant blossoms, the Saints began to put down roots in Commerce, Illinois. The Church of Jesus Christ of Latter-day Saints was also still "green," being only nine years old. Brigham Young, Heber C. Kimball and the other apostles were also "green," having been apostles only three years and having no modern role models to emulate. Missouri had been their proving ground. They passed with flying colors of charity and courage, defying murderous mobs to bring even the poorest Saints to safety.

The members of the Church of Jesus Christ fled the persecution of Far West, crossing the entire state of Missouri. After traveling more than 150 miles, some barefoot and poorly clad, these Saints stopped at the banks of the Mississippi, eventually crossing over either by canoeing through perilous ice chunks or by walking when the Mississippi River was completely frozen over.

In Quincy, Illinois, good souls took in so many Latter-day Saints that those being rescued outnumbered the population of Quincy three to one.[1]

The Saints were without means to provide any necessities. There was no shelter from the freezing weather, no guns with which to hunt or provide protection, no coats, coverings or food. Apostle Wilford Woodruff wrote:

> *I saw a great many of the Saints, old and young, lying in the mud and water, in a rainstorm, without tent or covering.... The sight filled my eyes with tears.*[2]

John Wood, a prosperous early settler of Quincy, sent relief supplies across the river. The residents of Quincy were so appalled at the plight of the incoming families that they issued proclamations for all citizens to care for and comfort the exiles. In his defense of Joseph Smith, the famous Quincy lawyer, Orville H. Browning (nephew to the gunsmith and inventor, Jonathan Browning) said:

ABOVE: *The Saints came to Commerce, Illinois, in the cold of winter, most without means to provide for their families.*

Great God! have I not seen it? Yes, my eyes have beheld the blood-stained faces of innocent women and children, in the drear winter, who had traveled hundreds of miles barefoot, through frost and snow, to seek a refuge from their savage pursuers. [3]

The first Mormons immigrating to the vicinity of Nauvoo were Israel Barlow and about thirty others. Here they met Dr. Isaac Galland, an eastern realtor, who claimed the fort and most of the available land near Montrose. He made the Church an attractive offer of land on both sides of the river, including 20,000 acres in Iowa for $2.00 an acre. Payment would be in twenty annual installments, interest free.

Joseph Smith recorded:

The place was literally a wilderness. The land was mostly covered with trees and bushes, and much of it was so wet that it was with utmost difficulty a footman could get through and totally impossible for teams. Commerce was so unhealthy, very few could live there; but believing that it might become a healthful place by the blessing of heaven to the saints, and no more eligible place presenting itself, I considered it wisdom to make an attempt to build up a city. [4]

On 24 April 1839, Joseph advised the brethren "who could do so, to go to Commerce and locate in Dr. Galland's neighborhood." It consisted of "one

ABOVE: *On the banks of the Mississippi near Commerce.*

stone house, three frame houses, and two block houses, which constituted the whole city of Commerce." [5]

Joseph recorded on Friday, May 10, 1839:

I arrived with my family…and took up my residence in a small log house on the bank of the river, about one mile south of Commerce City, hoping that I and my friends may here find a resting place for a little season at least. [6]

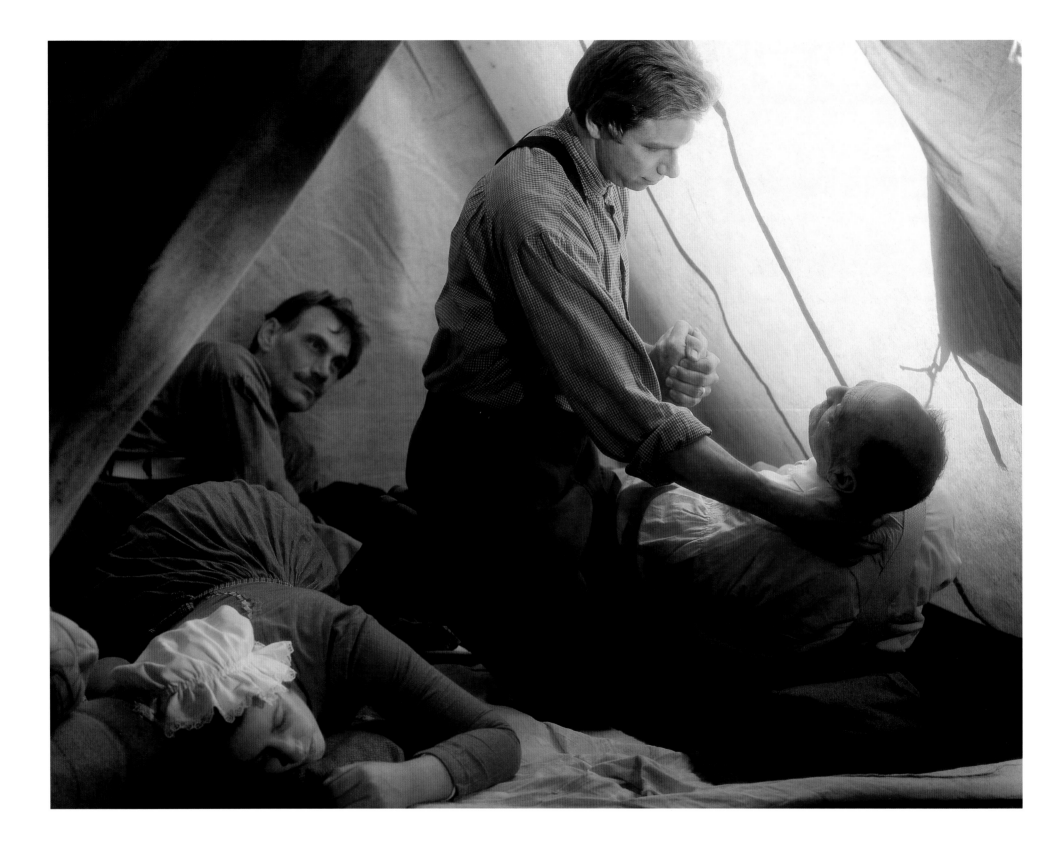

As the Saints settled on the undrained Commerce flats they were devastated by malaria. Only a handful of rough cabins stood on the Commerce property, and the Saints were housed only in tents and wagon covers. Joseph and Emma were in a tent also, having given their small log home to those most ill, whom they also cared for. On the morning of July 22, 1839, the Prophet arose from his own bed of sickness. Filled with the Spirit of the Lord, he went forth healing all who were afflicted.

After healing all the sick upon the bank of the river as far as the stone house, he called upon Elder Kimball and some others to accompany him across the river to visit the sick at Montrose. Many of the Saints were living there at the abandoned military barracks originally built by the U.S. Army in 1808 at Fort Des Moines. Among them were several of the Quorum of the Twelve, including its president, Brigham Young. Joseph healed him, and they then visited Wilford Woodruff, Orson Pratt and John Taylor, who joined them.

The four men accompanied Joseph to see Elijah Fordham, "who was supposed to be about breathing his last…. The Prophet…walked to [him], took hold of his right hand and spoke…. "Brother Fordham was unable to speak; his eyes were set in his head like glass, and he seemed entirely unconscious…." Joseph held his hand and looked into his

LEFT: A depiction of the Prophet Joseph healing those who were sick with malaria on July 22, 1839.
ABOVE: The swampy bank of the Mississippi. When the flatland was drained, the city became inhabitable.

ABOVE: A depiction of the twin girls who were healed by Wilford Woodruff. RIGHT: A facsimile of Joseph's red silk handkerchief.
FAR RIGHT: A beautiful site: engagements were a frequent occurrence here at the Stone Arch Bridge Scenic Turnout.

eyes in silence for a length of time. A change in [his] countenance…was soon perceptible to all present. His sight returned, and upon Joseph asking him if he knew him, [Elijah], in a low whisper, answered, 'Yes.'

"Joseph asked him if he had faith to be healed.

"Elijah answered, 'I fear it is too late; if you had come sooner I think I would have been healed.'

"The Prophet said, 'Do you believe in Jesus Christ?'

"He answered in a feeble voice, 'I do.'

"Joseph then stood erect, still holding his hand in silence several moments; then he spoke in a very loud voice, saying, 'Brother Fordham, I command you, in the name of Jesus Christ, to arise from this bed and be made whole.' … It seemed as though the house shook to its very foundations. [Elijah] arose from his bed and was immediately made whole. His feet were bound in poultices, which he kicked off;

then putting on his clothes, he ate a bowl of bread and milk, and followed the Prophet into the street."7

One year later Elijah Fordham would carve the baptismal font for the Nauvoo temple. He traveled with the Saints to Utah, where he died in 1880.

A man not of the Church of Jesus Christ who knew of the healings begged the Prophet to go with him and heal his twin infant daughters.

The Prophet could not go, but said he would send someone to heal them. Taking from his pocket a red silk handkerchief, he handed it to Elder Wilford Woodruff and requested him to go and heal the children. He told Elder Woodruff to wipe the faces of the children with the handkerchief, and they should be healed. This he did and they were healed. "As long as you keep that handkerchief," said Joseph, "it shall remain a league between you and me." Elder Woodruff kept it all his days. 8

BUILDING A "CITY BEAUTIFUL"

Cabins, crops, then culture sprouted in Nauvoo. Once the culvert was dug where the bluff met the flatland, rain no longer made swamps but a beautiful flowing creek instead, which ended at the Mississippi. Couples came to propose their engagement and plan their future. Nauvoo became the "Jewel of the Mississippi," as a gentleman from Boston wrote:

*No one can visit Nauvoo and come away without
a conviction that…the body of the Mormons were
an industrious, hard-working and frugal people.
In the history of the whole world there cannot be
found such another instance of so rapid a rise of
a city out of the wilderness, a city so well built,
a territory so well cultivated.*[1]

When settlers arrived in Nauvoo, many built log homes. These log dwellings were from one to three rooms, with a shallow attic for sleeping. They were often built in cob fashion, with clay and mortar chinks between the logs, and generally did not have floors, windows, or enough fireplaces to keep the home warm. Warren Foote, a Mormon schoolteacher, described an overnight visit to Nauvoo:

> *I awoke this morning and found myself buried in snow. The house we slepped [sic] in had no floor and was very open and the snow had blowed [sic] through the crevices and covered us up…. Many of the houses being very open the snow blowed into them and melting made it extremely disagreeable.* 2

It is estimated that there were over one thousand log cabins built in Nauvoo. William Oliver recorded in 1843 that the total cost to erect a log home eighteen by twenty feet was $239.77, or in current dollar values, about $10,000. Sally Randall first saw the home her husband had prepared for her and their children in that same year and recorded:

> *He has a lot with a log cabin on it and it is paid for. The house is very small but I think we can get along with it for the present. He had a table and three chairs. We have no bedsteads yet, but shall have soon.* 3

ABOVE: *A depiction of Warren Foote, waking up covered with snow in the Field Log Cabin.*
RIGHT: *Two reconstructed cabins are located next to the Lyon Drug on Hotchkiss Street.*

Charlotte Haven, a young non-Mormon, stayed in Nauvoo for almost a year. She described early Nauvoo to her family in a letter:

> *The houses are still of the rudest construction… mere shelters, many built of logs placed cob fashion, some of only one thickness of boards, and others of sod or mud, with seldom any plastering or floors, and minus chimneys, doors, and windows. [The impoverished Saints placed a funnel about the roof or through a side wall, and hung quilts over doors and windows.] You would think it impossible that human beings could inhabit such hovels…. In spite of their scanty clothing and midwinter prairie breezes that play so freely through their dwellings, these [children] look healthy and happy.* 4

When we consider the short time since the Mormons came here, and their destitution after having had every vestige of property taken from them, and after having undergone great suffering and persecution…, we cannot wonder that they have no fitter dwelling place and so few of the comforts of life.[5]

— Charlotte Haven

ABOVE: *The Joseph Smith Homestead (seen from the back) includes log, block and frame construction. The log cabin existed before Joseph and Emma moved in. It is estimated that approximately 2,000 homes were built in Nauvoo over a seven-year period. Of these, between 200–300 were brick and the remainder were either log or frame homes.* 6 RIGHT: *The pines at Nauvoo State Park.* FAR RIGHT: *A wood plane from the Nauvoo era.*

*T*he need for lumber to build Nauvoo was not easily met. The city that Joseph Smith envisioned required vast amounts of timber. Since the treeless prairies of Illinois did not furnish the wood needed, pine forests some five or six hundred miles north seemed the best source. So "a company of the brethren started for the pinery...for the purpose of procuring lumber for the Temple and Nauvoo House."[7]

After six months of effort in the pineries, the prophet copied an editorial from the *Times and Seasons* into his journal in April 1842:

> *A company was formed last fall to go to the pine country to purchase mills, and prepare and saw lumber for the Temple and the Nauvoo House, and the reports from them are very favorable; another company has started, this last week, to take their place and to relieve those that are already there: on their return they are to bring a very large raft of lumber....*[8]

The production of bricks became an extremely important part of the economic and social aspects of Nauvoo. Brick production and brick masonry employed hundreds. The spacious and more permanent homes and buildings provided for larger gatherings of all kinds.

"Making bricks began as four parts of clay were mixed with one part sand and just enough water to make 'brick dough.' The dough was then shaped in molds greased with lard and tallow. Damp bricks were fired for six to eight days in kilns heated to 2100 degrees Fahrenheit. It took thirty-three days from the mixing pond to the kiln before a single brick was ready to be sold for a half-cent." The average two-story dwelling required 40,000 bricks. 9

The *Neighbor* anticipated the manufacture of four million bricks in Nauvoo during the summer of 1845. The brick kilns were apparently burning around the clock. 10

ABOVE: The Simeon Dunn Home at the southwest corner of Parley and Hyde Streets. ABOVE RIGHT: A commemorative, modern-day souvenir brick from the Nauvoo Brickyard. FAR RIGHT: The interior of the reconstructed Webb Blacksmith Shop. A blacksmith stands in front of the forge hammering a hot iron horseshoe. It is estimated that there were as many as six blacksmith shops in Nauvoo.

Many people of Nauvoo were young, full of energy and possessed great craftsmanship. Every able person worked: Brigham Young worked as a carpenter and glazier, and Heber Kimball as a blacksmith and potter. Lucius Scovil was a contractor and baker; Calvin Pendleton was a physician, blacksmith and gunsmith.

Those without money for materials bartered for it. They erected hundreds of buildings, including shops for skilled craftsmen.

A report of Nauvoo in the *Millennial Star,* the Church's official newspaper in England, on June 10, 1841 said:

Everywhere we see men of industry with countenances beaming with cheerful content hurrying to their several occupations and scenes of labor. The sound of the axe, the hammer, and the saw, greet your ear in every direction, and others are springing up, and ere we are aware of it are filled with happy occupants. 11

Heber C. Kimball noted in the *Star,* September 10, 1841 after his return from a mission in England:

We built our houses in the woods [with] not a house within half a mile of us. Now the place, wild as it was at that time, is covered into a thickly populated village. 12

ABOVE: *The George Riser Boot Shop (Cheap Boot & Shoe Manufactory) was rebuilt on the original site and has only a 16-foot frontage.*
ABOVE RIGHT: *This pair of shoes, now on display in the Lyon Drug Store, are identical. They were not designed specifically for right and left feet so the shoes could be interchanged daily to wear evenly.*

George Riser and his wife, Christianna, were both German immigrants, but met and married in Ohio. An employee, Ebineezer Kerr, told them about the gospel. They sold their business and traveled to Nauvoo to meet the Prophet. On December 12, 1842, they cut a hole in the ice of the Mississippi and Joseph baptized them.

George and Christianna opened this boot shop, which employed five men. No shoes were made in advance. Various sized "lasts" were used as patterns and to fit the shoe upon during construction. Leather was chosen to fit the need of the shoe or boot, and cut with a large long-handled knife. The sewing was done with a boar-bristle needle with full arm motion called "whipping the cat."13 A thick cowhide was used for the sole, and a stamp cut out the heels. Heels were stacked, glued and nailed together to the height the customer requested. Prices varied from 75 cents for a pair of small child's shoes to five dollars for a pair of man's boots.

Sylvester Stoddard opened this Tin Shop on Main Street. Baptized in Kirtland in 1836, Sylvester served in the bishopric while living in Nauvoo and in 1844 served a mission to Maine. His family ran a successful business here at the Tin Shop and "were considered among the economically elite in Nauvoo."[14]

Because tin cannot tolerate high temperatures, it is used primarily as a coating for stronger metals, like iron. The more an object is coated, the greater will be its durability and difference in color.

Tin was used to construct the dome of the original Nauvoo Temple and to make the temple's weather vane. Other objects that were made of tin and sold at the tin smith were tin cups; a set of six sold for 37½ cents; a tin pan, 43 cents; and a tin bucket, 50 cents—a hefty price considering that an average day's labor netted one dollar.[15]

ABOVE: The Stoddard Tin Shop is on the west side of Main between Numson and Kimball Streets.
BELOW LEFT: The interior of the Tin Shop, displaying items of tin manufactured in Nauvoo.

The arrival of mail in Nauvoo brought news from the outside world and was an exciting event. It was probably carried once weekly on horseback. The best known postmaster, Sidney Rigdon, used the kitchen in his home as the post office from February 1841 to May 1844. A post office was built in town in 1845 by James Ivins.

ABOVE: The reconstructed Post Office is located on Main Street across from the Browning Gunsmith Home and Shop. LEFT: The interior of the Post Office.

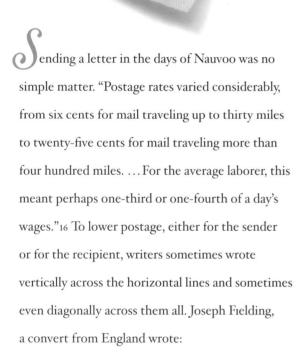

Sending a letter in the days of Nauvoo was no simple matter. "Postage rates varied considerably, from six cents for mail traveling up to thirty miles to twenty-five cents for mail traveling more than four hundred miles. ...For the average laborer, this meant perhaps one-third or one-fourth of a day's wages."16 To lower postage, either for the sender or for the recipient, writers sometimes wrote vertically across the horizontal lines and sometimes even diagonally across them all. Joseph Fielding, a convert from England wrote:

I would, with pleasure, write letters to many individuals in England and the Isle of Man, but I must beg to be excused; it would take more money than I can at present command. 17

There were no envelopes, so letters were folded and sealed with wax. The postmaster charged by

Photographed with permission of the Community of Christ, World Headquarters, Independence, Missouri

ABOVE: *This original Newel K. Whitney desk was given to Joseph Smith, III when the Whitney family left Nauvoo.* FAR LEFT: *This facsimile shows how letters were written in multiple directions to save on postage expense.* RIGHT: *The front of the Browning Gun Shop and Home.*

the number of sheets of paper as well as the distance the piece of mail had to travel.

After each piece was examined, postage was calculated and the amount due was written on the outside of the sheets. The sender could then pay for the postage but usually did not, knowing that curiosity would be too much to bear for the recipient, who would redeem the mail. Joseph Smith wrote this response to a less-than-friendly letter:

Dear Brother—I wish to inform my friends and all others abroad, that whenever they wish to address me through the post office, they will be kind enough to pay the postage on the same. My friends will excuse me in this matter, as I am willing to pay postage on letters to hear from them; but I am unwilling to pay for insults and menaces; consequently must refuse all unpaid.

Yours in the Gospel, Joseph Smith, Jun. 18

*J*onathan Browning's home is of unusual length for Nauvoo, approximately 75 feet as compared with other homes, which are 18–25 feet. Restored, it is a beautiful brick home, shop, cabin and store—a fitting monument to a great family, inventor and obedient Saint.

WILL MANUFACTURE
TO ORDER REVOLVING
RIFLES AND PISTOLS

JONATHAN BROWNING
GUNSMITH
BLACKSMITH & FARRIER

WILL ALSO MANUFACTURE
SLIDE GUNS FROM
5 TO 25 SHOOTERS

JONATHAN
BROWNING
HOME AND
GUN SHOP

$\mathcal{J}$onathan Browning was born in Brushy Fork, Sumner County, Tennessee, on October 22, 1805. He was interested in gunsmithing at an early age and learned soldering, brazing, welding, hand-forging and tempering. At 14, he asked for and received an old, rusted gun for helping a farmer for the week. Jonathan restored it so well that the farmer bought it back for four dollars.

Browning married his childhood sweetheart, Elizabeth Stalcup. In 1834, they moved to Quincy, Illinois, where he set up shop, had acquaintance with Abraham Lincoln and invented one of the earliest repeating rifles.

A Mormon came into his shop with a repair job and introduced Jonathan to the gospel. He read the Book of Mormon and was baptized. In 1843, they moved to Nauvoo with their business of making and repairing guns. Each rifle he made had the inscription, "Holiness to the Lord, Our Preservation," acknowledging God as the greatest protector.

He advertised, "The subscriber is prepared to manufacture, to order, improved Fire-arms, viz: revolving rifles and pistols; also slide guns, from 5 to 25 shooters."[19]

Upon leaving Nauvoo, Brigham Young would let Browning go no further than Kanesville, Iowa, knowing that his talents for gunsmithing were needed to help the pioneers as they moved west. Browning's son, John Moses Browning, built on what his father taught him. "His accomplishments are remarkable, whether they are measured by their innovations, their number, their duration, or their popularity."[20]

John Moses Browning "was issued 128 patents [for] some eighty firearm models. Well over thirty million designed guns have been produced to date by Winchester, Colt, Fabrique Nationale, Remington, Savage and others."[21]

FAR LEFT: *The back door of the Browning Gun Shop.* ABOVE: *The Byrds traded this cabin and home on the east side of Main Street with the Jonathan Browning family.* BELOW: *The Jonathan Browning slide repeating rifle with ingenious five-shot magazine was loved for its few parts and ease of operation.* Photo courtesy of the Union Station John M. Browning Firearms Museum in Ogden, Utah.

There were two newspapers printed weekly or semiweekly in Nauvoo. The *Times and Seasons* was published as an official Church publication, beginning in 1842 with a circulation of 2,000. "Subsidized by the Church, it had no need for advertisements and is therefore a rich deposit of Church history and doctrinal development in Nauvoo."[22] Its pages were filled with words of the Prophet Joseph and other general authorities.

A secular Nauvoo newspaper was founded by Joseph Smith's brother, William, and was first called the *Wasp*.

The printed word was greatly respected throughout the country, but its influence was especially powerful in Nauvoo, where the two publications provided a means of spiritual communication as well as a source of entertainment for its readers.

John Taylor, a member of the Quorum of the Twelve Apostles, became the editor of both papers in 1842. He enlarged the size of the *Wasp* and changed the name to the *Nauvoo Neighbor*.

FAR LEFT: *Depiction of John Taylor opening the Print Shop in the early morning hours.* LEFT: *A facsimile of Taylor's two publications.*
ABOVE: *Depiction of John Taylor, editor of* Times & Seasons *and the* Nauvoo Neighbor, *and George Q. Cannon, his nephew, whom Taylor raised after the death of George's parents. George apprenticed under Taylor at the Print Shop and later became the editor of the* Deseret News.

Two years later he would buy the entire printing establishment for $2,832. This price included the building, lot, press, bindery and foundry.[23]

The *Nauvoo Neighbor*, including its advertisements, today gives us very personal glimpses into the life of Nauvoo residents in the early 1840s.

On August 9, 1843, the *Neighbor* included some advice for single female readers:

Never blush, never apologize if found by young men in your homespun attire, stirring the coffee, washing the hearth, or rinsing the clothes…. Industrious habits are certainly the best recommendations you can bring to worthy young men who are seeking wives.[24]

On August 27, 1845, the *Neighbor* revealed something of the palate of many residents of Nauvoo:

ABOVE: Twenty to thirty of the same letter were kept in a box and each letter was typeset individually. Capital letters were kept in the "upper case" and small letters were in the lower (or bottom) cases.

On Saturday last, a large number of persons partook of a feast of melons, round a table 87 feet long in the attic story of the Temple. 25

The prophet Joseph and John Taylor were very loyal friends, and in 1843 the prophet Joseph wrote the following to John Taylor:

I believe you can do more good in the editorial department than preaching.... We have no one else we can trust the paper with, and hardly with you, for you suffer the paper to come out with so many mistakes. 26

Of greater concern to Taylor may have been simply keeping enough paper in stock, as the paper came by way of the Mississippi on a steamer. On November 13, 1844, the *Neighbor* explained that the paper was not able to meet production due to a "bad state of navigation, [etc.]" 27

The influence of printer's language can still be seen today. For example, John Taylor "missed the boat" when he failed to get the paper off the riverboat and it continued upstream. Decorative space holders were called "Ding Bats," indicating all show and no substance. When a column of type was complete, it was slid into a galley for a "dry run." A little ink was then rolled on the print and hand-pressed to check for mistakes.

It took a good printer 18 hours to set one newspaper page. It then took his apprentice 12 hours to put the type back into the case. The process of typesetting and running the paper through the press, hanging the wet page to dry, then taking it down and folding it took 30 hours per page.

Important publications were also printed in Nauvoo during this period. Some well-known authors' works include Heber C. Kimball's *Journal* in 1841, some books on poetry by Eliza R. Snow, and *The Collection of Sacred Hymns* by Emma Smith.

These books were typically purchased without a cover. The customer could then order the cover he or she preferred.

ABOVE: *Jonathan Browning lived in the center of activity in Nauvoo. A few blocks south are the Mansion House, the Nauvoo House and the Homestead of Joseph Smith; less than two blocks south stands the Brigham Young Home; across the street are the* Times and Seasons *buildings. A clear view of the temple can also be seen from the northeast corner of the Browning Home.*

$\mathcal{W}$indsor Lyon and his wife Sylvia Sessions used their brick building as both store and home. Windsor was practiced in herbal and botanical medicine and made the grounds of his store beautiful with the blooming herb gardens he grew. The store carried many items, such as dry goods, groceries, crockery, glass, hardware, books and stationery, paints and dyes, boots, shoes, military goods, etc.

Both Sylvia and her mother, Patty Sessions, were sought-after midwives, and Sylvia herself was a knowledgeable herbalist. Joseph Smith noted that "herbs and roots could be found to 'effect all necessary purposes' " for medicine. [28] So important were these herbs, that Thomas Bullock "packed up a medicine chest, [and] gathered some sage and dried it" for his journey west. [29]

LEFT: *Windsor and Sylvia Lyon opened a drugstore specializing in herbal and botanical medicine. They grew their medicinal herbs in gardens outside their shop. They also sold dry goods, groceries, crockery, glass, hardware, books, shoes and fabric.*
ABOVE: *Miniatures (or dolls) were dressed in the latest "Eastern Fashion," and changed seasonally. When women came to buy fabric, they could look at the doll, buy fabric and trims and create the latest fashions. Men's neckwear was also displayed.*

BELOW LEFT: *A mortar and pestle ground dried herbs to powder.*
LEFT: *Herbs were combined and made into a dough.*
This machine formed the dough into pills.
BELOW: *A red and blue stacked glass in a window represented*
an apothecary. The blue water represented blue blood and the
red represented the oxygenated, red blood.
FAR RIGHT: *A daily log was kept to record transactions of the*
day. The bottle at left was dye "for hair and beards." The other
bottle was a white rose triple extract guaranteed perfume.
A homemade bar of soap was also a valued commodity.

*L*yon Drug was really a "superstore" of the era. Groceries were obtained by cash or trade. A riverboat called *The Osprey* brought both supplies and people from over the ocean and up from Orleans. Sperm oil and other types of whale oil were carried there for filling lamps that gave light but no smoke. Pounded ash baskets, the most durable made, were sold there. There were witches' brooms, hearth brooms and whisk brooms.

A casual shopper could come in the morning, sit and play dominoes, observe the clientele, exchange news and gossip and stay warm by the stove.

Smoked whole turkeys with their feathers still on were hung next to a "brains tanned" buffalo hide. Jacquard woven blankets and loomed rugs may have sat by a pile of vegetables left as trade. In the corner by the window, in a vertical case behind glass, were guns, knives, bayonets, muskets, powder, balls, wadding, caps and shells—all the necessary tools of the frontier to defend one's family and provide for them.

Prominently displayed on front shelves was pottery from Staffordshire potters who were hoping to manufacture their designs in Nauvoo. Imported glassware included "Strawberryware," "Copperlustreware" and "Transferware."

A customer might also purchase sunglasses, eyeglasses, silverware, men's suspenders, canteens or a can for carrying documents. Behind the counter was a whole case of spices and herbs for flavorings and medicinal use. Vanilla, sassafras, sage, orange, cinnamon, celery, oregano, rosemary and chicory root all waited to be weighed on an 1840's scale.

Finally, on one of the shelves, a tooth extractor rested alongside an ivory-handled toothbrush. Most people just used a twig for tooth hygiene, which resulted in the need for the tooth extractor in later years. It is also interesting to note that the only hair dye on the shelf was for men and their beards. Apparently a grizzled gray beard was undesirable in the 1840s.

*G*ingerbread cookies were only one of the delicacies available at the The Scovil Bakery and Confectionary, which was one of four bakeries in Nauvoo. Although small, it contained two bustle ovens; one attached to the main building and another located behind. A bustle oven was built to extend out of the house, resembling a woman's bustle skirt, which fashionably ballooned out. This allowed more room in the building, and did not heat up the building as much in the summer time.

Scovil Bakery Gingerbread Cookies*

1 Cup sugar   ¾ Cup oil or lard
1 Cup molasses   ½ Cup hot water

Combine above ingredients. Use the hot water to rinse the molasses out of the cup.

Whisk together and mix into ingredients above:
1 tsp. soda   ½ tsp. salt
1 tsp. cinnamon   1 heaping tsp. ginger
6–7 cups of flour (use ⅓ whole wheat flour)

Refrigerate dough until chilled. Roll out and cut with cookie cutter. Bake at 350° for 10 minutes.

The *Nauvoo Neighbor* once advertised wedding cakes, ranging in price, from $1–25. With the average salary at about one dollar per day and a loaf of bread costing three cents, a $25 wedding cake would be "comparable to over $1,000 today."[30] Certainly such a cake would be beyond the means of any Nauvoo resident, but the advertisement certainly would have grabbed the attention of its reader.

Although sweets, like dried fruit, jellies, pastes and conserves, were often purchased at Scovil's Bakery, candy was a great luxury. Most parents felt candy was not healthful for children, and "sugar was kept locked in small chests to remove temptation."[31] Honey was used for sweetening and came from beehives scattered about the gardens of Nauvoo. At one time straw-rope hives (seen above) were used, but because it was difficult to remove the honey and the wax from the hives without killing the bees, new wooden hives were used to replace them.[32]

Recipe used courtesy of Nauvoo Restoration, Inc.

*F*or three or four miles upon the river and about the same distance back in the country, Nauvoo presents a city of gardens, ornamented with the dwellings of those who have made a covenant by sacrifice, and are guided by revelation, an exception to all other societies upon the earth. 33

PREVIOUS PAGE LEFT: *The Scovil Bakery with bustle oven has been reconstructed on the original foundation. It is possible that the bakery had a second story.* PREVIOUS PAGE RIGHT: *A rope beehive from the Blacksmith Shop.* ABOVE: *The front of the Browning Gun Shop overflows with beautiful flora of every type and color during the summer months.* RIGHT: *Inside of the Brigham Young Home. Depiction of Brigham's wife, Mary Ann, and her son. Early fall was a busy time for women, who preserved food to sustain life through the winter. Apples were favorites to peel and core for pies and desserts, to dry on racks, press into cider, or cook into preserves or apple butter.*

SUSTAINING A FAMILY

Nauvoo was a place where families regained strength.

*We were…glad of a resting place out of the reach of those who had sought our lives…. We were truly a thankful and humble people.*1 — Sarah Rich

Women fixed their homes, planted and cultivated gardens, bore and nurtured children, cared for animals, harvested, preserved and prepared food, nursed the sick and made clothing and household items. The Brownings had a rocking box that rocked a cradle and churned butter. The Woodruffs had a rocking bench with railing for a baby to sleep in while mother held a child or did handwork. The men plowed and built barns, outhouses, fences, wagons and carriages. They made furniture, ran businesses employing the family, led the Church and community and went on missions. Children had morning and evening chores and attended school, if their family could spare them.

$\mathcal{B}$read-making in Nauvoo began in the morning by making a fire in the oven. While the oven warmed, the ingredients were measured, mixed and kneaded. The dough was placed in a dough riser with a bowl of warm water. In about two hours, when the baker could hold a hand in the oven for about five seconds without drawing it out, the temperature was approximately 350 degrees—ideal for baking bread. The ashes were removed and saved for soap-making. Cornmeal was spread on the oven bottom, and the bread dough was placed on a wooden "peel" and slid into the oven to bake.

The top part of the baked loaf was the most delicious, thus comes the term "upper crust." This was saved for special guests. The middle section of the bread was for the family, and the bottom section, which was slightly burned, was given to the hired help.

ABOVE LEFT: *A woman kneads bread in the Nauvoo Living Center.* ABOVE: *A brick bustle oven typical of the time. Burning logs were removed with long tongs, and a shovel, scraper and whisk broom scooped out the ash. The wooden oven door was soaked all night, then replaced, to keep heat in and give moisture to the baked product.* RIGHT: *Inside the Family Living Center one can see a wood box to store finished candles before use. It was nailed shut to keep vermin from eating the tallow. The tin candle save was used to store used candles overnight. A lump of beeswax melted and added to the tallow helped the candle burn brighter and longer.* FAR RIGHT: *A mousetrap used during the Nauvoo period.*

Candles provided light in the evening, enabling women to sew or spin and the men to work or read before bedtime. Making candles was an essential, several-day task that required the entire family.

"Bits of tallow (animal fat) were saved and melted down in large kettles. Homemade wicks or store-bought cotton twists were tied to sticks and repeatedly dipped and cooled until they were of the proper size. Faster, neater candles could be turned out six to twenty-four at a time with candle molds."[2]

At bedtime, it was often the children's task to place the candles in a metal "candle save," or box lined with straw. Only a tight lid could protect the candles from mice who enjoyed feasting on the tallow.

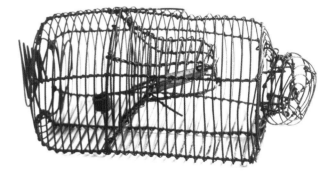

SUSTAINING A FAMILY

LEFT: *This method of candlemaking required thirty to forty dippings to make a candle that would burn 25–30 hours.*
ABOVE: *A flax spinning wheel.*
BELOW: *A woman's summer bonnet. Reeds kept the fabric away from the woman's hair and skin for ventilation.*
RIGHT: *A display in the Family Living Center shows the different stages of wool preparation.*
FAR RIGHT: *This iron weighed between eight and ten pounds. It was a labor-saving device as only the inside "iron" part ever touched the fire or ashes and was safely "buttoned-up" inside, retaining heat longer while the exterior "iron" remained ash-free.*

Making yarn from wool was labor-intensive. After the sheep were sheared and the fleece cleaned (sometimes washed in the river and laid on bushes to dry) it was carded and drawn out into yarn either on a spinning wheel or a drop spindle (pictured in photo above at the extreme left by the bottles).

After a day of spinning, in order to know how much yarn was spun, the husband held his hands 18 inches apart while the spinner wrapped the yarn around his hands. One wrap was one yard. A nifty invention called a "husband saver" wrapped the yarn around a spindle equaling one yard each.

Yarn was dyed with organic materials such as golden rod, sumac, walnut hulls, shells and tree barks. A mordant set the dye. Depending upon the mordants used—such as salt, alum, vinegar, cream of tartar or copper sulfate— various tones of color could be achieved.

LEFT: *This unique butter churn is found in the Browning Home.*
ABOVE: *A Betty lamp hangs on a fireplace mantle.*
BELOW LEFT: *Quilt by modern-day sisters of Nauvoo with center piece "Sisters pieced together, Stitched with charity, Colored with friendships, and Bound with love."*

*T*he Browning Home contains a favorite furniture arrangement of chair, knitting basket and rocking butter churn/cradle. A busy Jonathan Browning may have had this rocking device built so that he could keep busy with his shop while Elizabeth put the cream into the inside compartment, placed the cradle with baby securely on top, and sat in her

chair knitting, rocking the device with her foot and humming a lullaby to the precious cargo atop the labor-saving contraption.

A Betty lamp (seen above) was a portable lamp, like a flashlight, with a reservoir for grease or oil at the bottom and a twist of cotton in the center for a wick. These lamps hung over chair backs for light for reading or sewing, or were stuck in chinks on walls or between fireplace stone, to shine into stew pots cooking on the hearth. A lighted Betty lamp in the window in the evening signaled that the family was ready to receive visitors.

In the fall, or harvest time, the children helped sack potatoes and load them for market. The vegetables that were kept for family use were either stored in dirt cellars or pitted for winter. It was not unusual for the women and children to work in the fields and barnyard. Many women on the farms worked with the men to help get their land under cultivation.

Children helped to sustain the family as soon as they were old enough. "Starting at age four, the children started learning farm labor, working with animals, planting and harvesting, milking, butchering, and so on."[3]

Taking care of the cows included churning the cream to make butter—a long, drawn-out process at times. Children's arms would grow tired and they would "spell" each other off, taking turns with the churning.

A large quantity of butter had to be made for market on Saturdays. Every woman who made butter to sell considered it an art and prided herself on her reputation for making the finest butter.

Boys and girls carried lunches and fresh-churned buttermilk to the men in the fields. Older boys and girls worked in the fields with the men, planting potatoes, sowing seed by hand and raking hay.

ABOVE LEFT: Milking a cow on the Hasek Farm in Nauvoo.
ABOVE RIGHT: A butter churn.
ABOVE: A kitten hopes for a few drops of leftover milk.

An annoying problem during the summer months was flies. Without window screens, "flies migrated freely between stables and outdoor refuse to the insides of homes and food…. Children took turns "minding the flies" at mealtime, chasing them from the table area with a branch or a paper duster…." The invention of screens was a major advancement for sanitation, comfort and well-being. 4 Children were well regarded. An Englishman remarked of children in America: "There are no children in our sense of the term…only little men and women…. The merest boy will give his opinion upon the subject of conversation among his seniors; and he expects to be listened to and is."5

straight-backed, wooden arm chairs were built to catch heat from the fire, making them comfortably warm in the winter. This child's potty, pictured below, would be especially inviting to cold little bottoms, facilitating easy and fast potty training.

The "Fox and Geese" game was played similar to Checkers. Old and young alike enjoyed the game together.

LEFT: Children in Nauvoo wore clothing that was practical and comfortable. Many children, like their parents before them at their age, wore no underclothing. ABOVE: This wooden Noah's Ark was carefully carved to include unicorns. ABOVE RIGHT: Tiny leather shoes for an infant. RIGHT: Doll made from cloth and leather. BELOW CENTER: A child's "potty." BELOW LEFT: The game "Fox and Geese" is played similar to today's Checkers, but with fewer pieces than shown. Pictured is a game of Solitaire played on a Fox and Geese board.

Nauvoo was a young city, with most homeowners in their twenties or thirties. Children were a part of almost every household and usually had

a few toys and some children's furniture, which were simple and practical. The hand-carved wooden Noah's Ark set with animals going two-by-two was a favorite. It was also a Sunday quiet toy.

Placed in front of a blazing fireplace,

*I*n an 1838 message the First Presidency told the members of the Church:

> *One of the principle objects then, of our coming together, is to obtain the advantages of education; and in order to do this, compact society is absolutely necessary.* 6

It is probable that there were as many as twenty different common schools established in Nauvoo. "Of the eighty or so schoolteachers in Nauvoo between 1839 and 1846, approximately half were women."7 And at least half the students enrolled in Nauvoo schools were girls. 8

Brigham Young said:

> *We believe that women are useful not only to sweep houses, wash dishes, make beds and [rear] babies, but they should stand behind the counter, study law or physics, or become good bookkeepers and be able to do the business in any counting house.* 9

Children were only able to attend school for a few months at a time, usually in the colder months when they were not needed to do chores at home. An ad for subscription schools that appeared in The *Nauvoo Neighbor* indicated that subjects taught included geography, grammar, composition, philosophy, Greek, Latin, Spanish, French, chemistry, mathematics and music. 10

LEFT: *The front of the Calvin Pendleton Home and School.* ABOVE: *This small room was used for teaching children of many ages.*
ABOVE RIGHT: *Replicas of the McGuffey Readers are available today.*

"The classroom itself was furnished with crudely-made backless benches, a separate writing table and bench where the students could work with their copybooks, another table that served as the teacher's desk, a fireplace or stove, perhaps a hand-bell, occasionally a blackboard, and the indispensable water pail. Boys and girls…sat on opposite sides of the room. …Students ranged in age from five or six to marriageable youth…."11

The popular McGuffey Readers were probably used as the reading primers to grade four. These books are still available today.

For adults, the University of Nauvoo existed only in a few scattered classes. Lyceums and debating societies helped prepare participants for missionary and civic service.

A "membership lending library" contained 200 donated books on "science, world religion, history and literature."12

ABOVE: *The reconstructed Calvin Pendleton Home and School. Born in 1811 in Maine, Calvin Pendleton went to medical school in Ohio. Calvin came to Nauvoo in 1839 and used quinine for malaria with great success, giving his medical skills without charge. He learned the trade of blacksmith and gunsmith from Jonathan Browning, and also began a subscription school to contribute literacy to Nauvoo.* RIGHT: *A view through the trees of the Seventies Hall.*

The second floor of the Seventies Hall housed the Nauvoo Library and Museum of "curiosities" brought back from missions. Local and visiting artists also exhibited their paintings. Townspeople donated 675 books to the library for cultural improvement of the citizens.

Joseph Young, Brigham's elder brother, directed the building of the Seventies Hall with John D. Lee as chief secretary. Labor and materials were donated, as Lee records,

> *…when I could get a contract to take lumber from the river, as rafts would land in the city…the portion of the lumber that we got for our pay we piled up for the building. In this way we got all the lumber needed. The bricks we made ourselves….* 13

Early in 1844, when the 40-foot-long west wall was up 9 feet, a tornado blew it down, smashing the flooring. The Seventies were discouraged and considered abandoning the project. Brigham suggested they rebuild it, making the wall one brick thicker. They returned to work.

On December 27, 1844, the first of seven dedicatory services was held. The building would provide opportunities for future missionaries to improve teaching and preaching skills. It also was used for Sunday meetings, schools, lectures, etc.

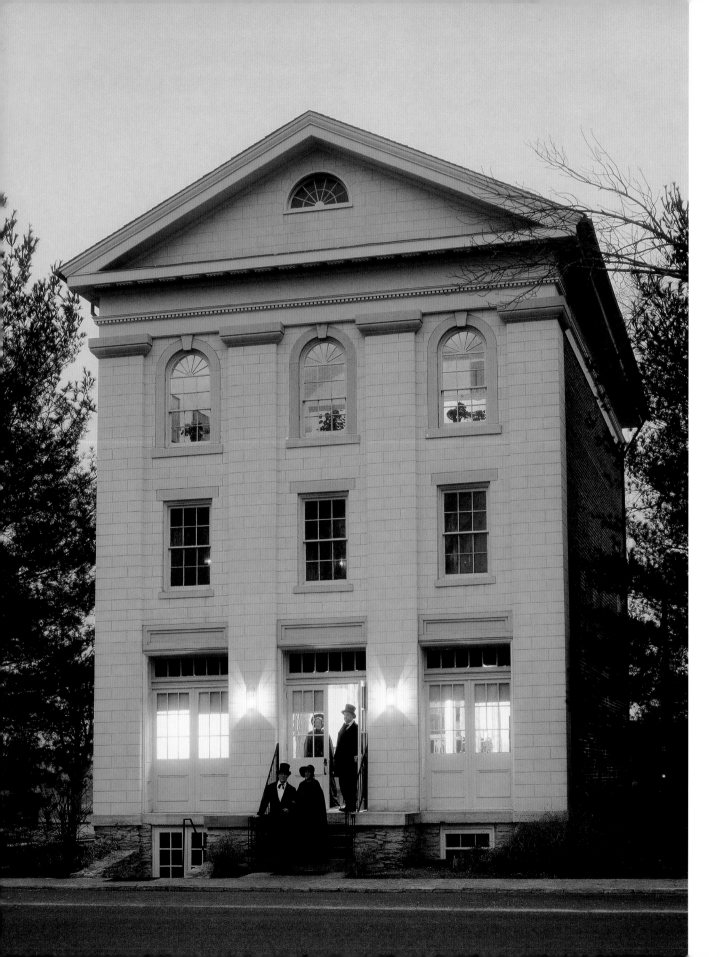

$\mathcal{M}$usic was an important part of Nauvoo life and was performed and enjoyed in this building, the Cultural Hall. Here, choirs were invited to sing, and Captain Pitt's Brass Band played stirring anthems and Church hymns. New hymns introduced there included "A Poor Wayfaring Man of Grief," Joseph's favorite.

The Cultural Hall was used for dancing, however, not everyone enjoyed the talent of dancing. Parley Pratt had some difficulty with his "two left feet." Orson Hyde once "observed Parley standing in the figure … making no motion particularly, only up and down. Says I, '…Why don't you move forward?' Says he, 'When I think which way I am going, I forget the step; and when I think of the step, I forget which way to go.' "14

This building was also used as a Masonic Hall, encouraging friendships with state political leaders.

PREPARING A PEOPLE

*B*righam Young, John Taylor, Wilford Woodruff
and Lorenzo Snow were all residents of Nauvoo,
and all became Presidents of the Church. They were
called on missions to England when they and their
families were destitute and gravely ill. Each man was
willing to serve, though it was almost impossible for
him to begin. Faith was demonstrated by beginning
the journey. They listened to the Spirit and miracles
were seen. Gifts of the Spirit were shared. Thousands
were baptized and came to Nauvoo. The Saints in
their poverty supported their missionaries and families.
For the Saints, accepting the Lord's callings and commandments with faith prepared them to become not
only His leaders but also like Him—charitable, wise,
patient and happy.

Erastus Snow married Artemesia Beman on December 13, 1838, during the winter exodus from Missouri. They moved to Nauvoo in the summer and were immediately sent on a mission to Salem, Massachusetts. There, they rented a home from Nathaniel Ashby, a shoemaker with ten children whom they had helped convert to the Church. Artemesia's father passed away in Nauvoo while she was in Salem, and she inherited a piece of property two blocks east of the Prophet's home.

Erastus and Artemesia sold the southeast corner of the property to the Ashbys for $500, who followed them to Nauvoo. The Snows had the contractor double their new home, creating mirror images with a wall separating them. The brickwork is some of the best in Nauvoo, and the house rests on a strong foundation. The large rooms on the first floor each had a grand cooking fireplace. The houses also have clothes closets with wooden pegs for hanging clothes, which was uncommon for their time.

The Snows were in their home for only two years. During that time Erastus operated a mercantile business in partnership with Parley P. Pratt.

The Ashby family didn't leave Nauvoo until 1846. Until then, they cared for pregnant wives of leaders who had gone ahead, including Bishop Hunter's and Brigham Young's wives.

PREVIOUS PAGE FAR LEFT: The Cultural Hall in the evening after a performance. PREVIOUS PAGE LEFT: Gentleman's top hat.
PREVIOUS PAGE RIGHT: Two missionaries pray in the mist of early morning before leaving Nauvoo. ABOVE: The Ashby and Snow Duplex.

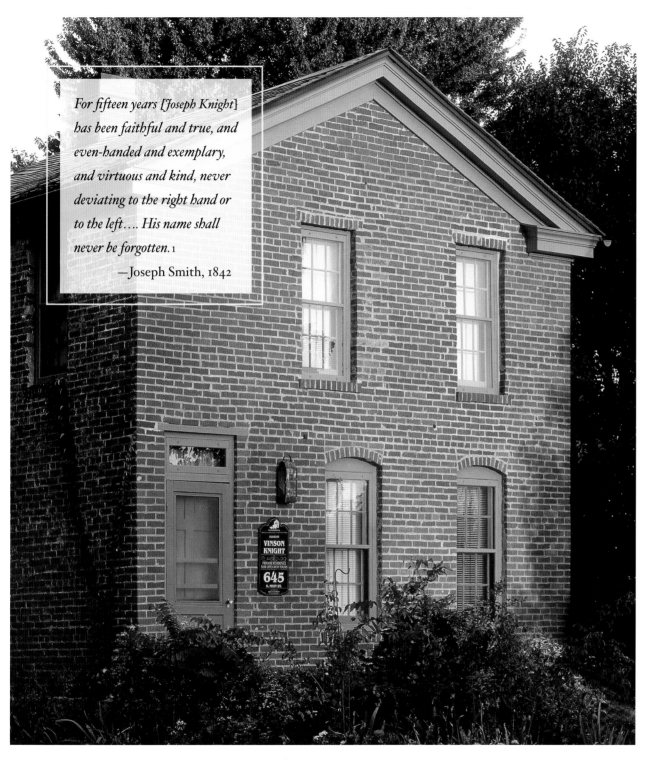

ABOVE: *The Vinson Knight Home. Vinson, of no relation to Joseph Knight, was taught the gospel by Joseph Smith and Parley P. Pratt in March of 1834 and was baptized later that fall. In 1841 he was ordained as the Presiding Bishop of the Church in Nauvoo.*

The Knight family of Nauvoo accepted the restored gospel shortly after Joseph Smith's family. At age twenty, Joseph Smith had worked for Joseph Knight in Colesville, New York, beginning a life-long friendship. The Knight family represented one-third of the sixty people attending the first meeting the day the Church was organized.

Father [Joseph] Knight loaned Joseph his wagon the night he got the plates for The Book of Mormon. Though not a wealthy man, he furnished Joseph and Emma with money, shoes, grain, potatoes, mackerel and paper for writing. "Then they went to work, and had provisions enough to last till the translation was done."2

Nine sections of the Doctrine and Covenants were written mentioning the Knights. And, still in use today, Knight Street in Nauvoo memorializes Joseph Smith's and the Saints' esteem for the Knights.

After crossing the Mississippi to bring his family west with the Saints, Newel Knight [son of Joseph Knight] recorded:

My heart swelled, for I beheld at a glance, from the eminences where I stood, the noble works of Joseph, the Prophet and Seer, and Hyrum his patriarch, with whom I had been acquainted, even from their boyhood, I knew their worth, and mourned their loss. 3

ABOVE: *A depiction of Bathsheba and George A. Smith in their early marriage. Photo taken at the reconstructed Sessions Cabin, named for David and Patty Bartlett Sessions.* RIGHT: *A photo of George A. Smith.*

Bathsheba Wilson Bigler Smith sent her husband, George A., on two missions within the first two years of their marriage. They had first met in Virginia, where he was serving a mission, and Bathsheba's family joined the Church. They pledged that "with the blessings of the Almighty in preserving us, in three years from this time, we will be married."[4] Following his return from a mission in England, Bathsheba wrote, "On the 25th of July, 1841, I was united in holy marriage to George Albert Smith, the then youngest member of the quorum of the twelve apostles."[5]

Following their wedding, the young couple lived with the Smith family for four weeks before moving into their first home, a rented log cabin with a leaky roof and a chimney that smoked. With stout hearts the newlyweds knelt at their bedside and thanked God for his blessings in bringing them together. Soon they found an unfinished log home to rent. It had no glass in the windows, so Bathsheba hung blankets up to keep the cold out and to provide some privacy.

They moved another time. This particular home was "the worst-looking house we had yet lived in" but had "the desirable qualities of neither smoking nor leaking."[6]

They soon purchased land and began building a two-story frame home. Anxious to have a permanent home, especially since Bathsheba was nearly nine months pregnant, they moved into the unfinished structure. Twelve days later, on July 7, 1842, George A. Smith, Jr., was born. Bathsheba not only began to care for her new son but also became responsible for completing the work on the home when her husband was called on another mission.

Bathsheba wrote to her husband:

When I get a letter first, all the rest come to hear it. The brethren's wives have all been to see me this week.[7]

It was perhaps fortunate that Bathsheba did not know that her 22-year-old husband, traveling with Brigham Young and Heber C. Kimball, was so ill that he temporarily lost his eyesight.

ABOVE: Bathsheba and George A. Smith's first cabin may have looked something like the Browning Cabin, located behind the Browning Building.

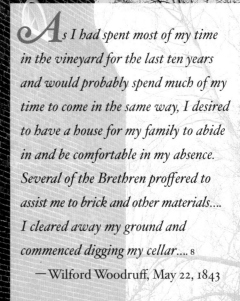

As I had spent most of my time in the vineyard for the last ten years and would probably spend much of my time to come in the same way, I desired to have a house for my family to abide in and be comfortable in my absence. Several of the Brethren proffered to assist me to brick and other materials.... I cleared away my ground and commenced digging my cellar.... 8

—Wilford Woodruff, May 22, 1843

Smith preach, teach, or prophesy, I always felt it my duty to write it; I felt uneasy and could not eat, drink, or sleep until I did write; and my mind has been so exercised upon this subject that when I would go home and sit down and write the whole sermon, almost word for word and sentence by sentence as it was delivered, and when I had written it it was taken from me, I remembered it no more. This was the gift of God to me. 12

Wilford kept a diary for over sixty-three years, a meticulous multivolume work covering nearly the entire history of the Church in the nineteenth century. He was appointed to be an apostle in 1839, and later became the fourth President of the Church.

𝒲ilford Woodruff married Phoebe Carter when he was thirty in Kirtland in 1837. "On the way to [Far West] Phoebe became so ill that she seemed dead. Quickly Wilford anointed her with oil, blessed her, and commanded her spirit to reenter her body. The results were miraculous, and she was able to continue the journey three days later."9

In 1839, they lived in the army barracks across the river from Nauvoo. Wilford records:

Early upon the morning of the 8TH of August, I arose from my bed of sickness, laid my hands upon the head of my sick wife... and blessed her. I then departed from the embrace of my companion, and left her almost without food or the necessaries of

life. She suffered my departure with the fortitude that becomes a saint.... 10

Wilford left on a mission to England. In the first three months he baptized over 200 people in Herefordshire. During an 18-month period, he helped bring over 1,800 souls into the Church.

Wilford suffered an unusual number of illnesses and accidents during his lifetime. A few were: "He survived the wreck of a speeding train, nearly drowned, [and] was both frozen and scalded.... He explained his preservation as a divine approval of his record keeping."11

I have had this spirit and calling... since I first entered this Church. ...Whenever I heard Joseph

FAR LEFT: *The Woodruff home was sold two years after its completion for only $675. The next day Wilford bought two wagons for $130. They left Nauvoo two weeks later on April 29, 1846.* ABOVE LEFT: *Paintings of Wilford and Phoebe during the Nauvoo period.* ABOVE: *Wilford Woodruff used this trunk for eight missions. He carried food, his scriptures, notes, books, journal, ink & quill, a change of clothing and a top hat.*

Heber C. Kimball, a potter and blacksmith, left his family to serve mission after mission, praying for the Lord to care for his family. Returning to Nauvoo in July 1841, he continued to spend most of his time as a minister to the Saints. When he returned from his mission in England, he was very surprised at the growth of the city.

*There were not more than thirty buildings in the city when we left about two years ago, but at this time there are twelve hundred; and hundreds of others in progress....*13

He also commented to family and friends:

*We landed in Nauvoo on the 1st of July and when we struck the dock I think there were about three hundred Saints there to meet us, and a greater manifestation of love and gladness I never saw before.*14

In 1843, Heber was called to go on a mission to the Eastern States. When he returned, he and his wife, Vilate, began to build a home. They were only to live in it four months.

Heber and Vilate were childhood sweethearts and their love for each other never failed:

July 28, 1843, I received three letters—one from my dear Vilate, one from my son Wm., and [daughter] Helen. How precious to hear from my dear wife and children whom I love, and prize above all other things here on Earth,....

*O God...spare the Love of my Youth that we may be one in all of our days and come forth in the Eternal worlds together with our dear children and friends. Amen.*15

Vilate wrote to Heber:

I have read [your letter] over and over with tears in my eyes; the feelings expressed therein [are] worth more to me than words could be without them.... It is one week yesterday since I closed a letter to you; although I have not spoken to you for a week, yet you have not been out of my mind many moments at a time when I was awake; and when I am asleep, I often dream about you.... My bosom friend, the love of my youth, gladly do I retire from the busy cares

*of life to spend a few moments in silent conversation to you.*16

Heber once remarked on the nature of God:

*I am perfectly satisfied that my Father and my God is a cheerful, pleasant, lively, and good-natured Being. Why? Because I am cheerful, pleasant, lively, and good-natured when I have His Spirit. That is one reason why I know; and another is—the Lord said through Joseph Smith, 'I delight in a glad heart and a cheerful countenance' [D&C 59:15]. That arises from the perfection of His attributes; He is a jovial, lively person, and a beautiful man.*17

I am glad the time of our exodus has come; I have looked for it for years.... There may be individuals who will look at their pretty houses and gardens and say, "it is hard to leave them"; but I tell you, when we start, you will put on your knapsacks, and follow after us. 18

—Heber C. Kimball

ABOVE: *This was the first adequate home the Kimballs had after twelve years of marriage. It is Federal Style, rectangular, brick, with double chimneys. Door and window openings are beautifully scaled with a fan window above the front door. An inscription stone above the balcony reads "H.C.K." Heber worked on it; but, it was also built with the donated labor of the Saints. This home was the first to be reconstructed in Nauvoo by Dr. LeRoy Kimball, the first President of Nauvoo Restoration, Inc. The style of the home was chosen by Dr. Kimball.* LEFT: *A drawing of Heber C., Vilate Kimball, and one of their children hangs in the Kimball home.*

ABOVE: The Brigham Young Home was first built as a two-story without the wings. They were added later as Brigham needed a conference room to seat the Twelve and more. ABOVE RIGHT: Photos of Mary Ann Young (taken after the Nauvoo period) and her husband, Brigham Young. Images reproduced courtesy of Church Archives, The Church of Jesus Christ of Latter-day Saints and © Intellectual Reserve, Inc.

Emmeline B. Wells, described Mary Ann's arrival that cold winter day:

"With her baby Alice in her arms, almost fainting with cold and hunger, and dripping wet with the spray from crossing the river.... I tried to persuade her to stay, but she refused, saying, 'the children at home are hungry too.' I shall never forget how she looked, shivering with cold and thinly clad. I kept the baby while she went to the tithing office. She came back with a few potatoes and a little flour, for which she seemed very grateful, and taking her baby with her parcels…weak as she was from ague and fever, wended her way back to the river bank. [21]

Aware of her need, Brigham wrote to his wife, Mary Ann:

I understand you have had hard work to get anything for yourself and family to make you comfortable. This I do not hear from you but from others…. My heart feels tender towards you, when I realize your patience and willingness to suffer in poverty and do everything you can for my children and for me to go and do the thing the Lord requires of me…. [22]

You say in your letter little Mary Ann cried the other night and did not want to go to bed till she had kneeled down and prayed for Father; bless the little creature. How I want to see her. [23]

𝓑righam Young was called as an apostle on Saturday, February 14, 1835. He later said:

Some of the knowing ones marvelled when we [Heber Kimball and I] were called to the Apostleship. It was indeed a mystery to me; but when I considered what consummate blockheads they were, I did not deem it so great a wonder. When they would meet brother Kimball and myself, their looks expressed, "What a pity!" Then I would think, You may, perhaps, make tolerably good men after a while; but I guess that you will tumble out by-and-by, just as they did: they could not stay in the Gospel net, they were so big and grew so fast; they became larger than the ship and slid overboard. [19]

Brigham Young, Wilford Woodruff and their families arrived in Commerce on May 18, 1839. Then the two apostles assisted others who were seeking shelter across the river at the abandoned barracks at Fort Des Moines.

On September 14, 1839, ten days after his wife, Mary Ann, delivered a baby girl, Brigham left for England. A month later, "her own means exhausted, Mary Ann Young one day left the older girls with the rest of the children while she crossed the Mississippi in an open boat, her baby bundled tight against the cold. She hoped to obtain food from the Nauvoo bishops." [20]

Mary Ann wrote back to her missionary husband:

I feel the Lord is good. I think we have learned quite a lesson since you left home. That is to trust in the Lord…. That is a great thing. I long to see you at home once more My Dear Husband. 24

On July 9, 1841, Brigham Young returned from his missionary service in England. He quickly went to work, "draining, fencing, and cultivating [his] lot, building a…shed for [his] cow, chinking and otherwise fixing [his] house." He also built a cellar. 25

May 31, 1843, Brigham records,

I moved out of my log cabin into my new brick house, which was 22′ x 16′, two stories high, and a good cellar under it, and felt thankful to God for the privilege of a house. 26

This was Brigham and Mary Ann's first brick home. They joyfully moved in with their seven children, including Mary and Vilate from Brigham's first wife, Joseph, 8, Brigham Jr. and Mary Ann (twins), 6, Alice, 3, and Luna, 9 months. A large downstairs room with its cooking hearth and "bustle oven" served as kitchen, dining room and the "keeping" center of family activities.

Later that year, little Mary was attacked by a severe cholera outbreak that took her life.

ABOVE: *Because of the high water table, Brigham Young built his root and fruit cellar above ground. He made the walls two bricks thick and put limestone on the ground. The ground was then covered by a wood floor.*

*J*ohn Taylor grew up in England, greatly interested in religion. He immigrated to Canada where he met, courted and married Leonora Cannon, ten years his senior.

Leonora took in a struggling missionary, Parley Pratt, who had been promised by Heber C. Kimball that he "would find a people prepared for the fulness of the gospel."[27] The Taylors copied eight of Brother Pratt's sermons, compared them with their own Bible and rejoiced. They and members of their study group joined the Church. John said, "I did it with my eyes open, I counted the cost; I looked upon it as a life-long job and I considered that I was not only enlisted for time, but for eternity."[28]

John presided over the LDS Church in Canada, and then came to Nauvoo, only to be called on a mission to his native home. He left Leonora and their three children, all sick with malaria. Leonora wrote to her husband, "I never needed more grace, patience or your prayers than I do at present."[29] At the end of the letter the children drew "smudgy circle 'kisses'" for their father.

John, who also had malaria as he began his mission, artistically created his own letterhead with, "My Dear Nora" included in the design.

Returning to Nauvoo, he served on the city council, was editor of the *Times and Seasons* and *Nauvoo Neighbor*, and along with Willard Richards, survived the martyrdom of Joseph Smith at the Carthage Jail. Here, John comfortingly sang, "A Poor Wayfaring Man of Grief" twice at the Prophet's request. He was wounded five times and left nearly dead under a dirty mattress. His pocket watch stopped a bullet, saving his life.

John Taylor became the third President of The Church of Jesus Christ of Latter-day Saints.

Jennetta Richards was baptized in England in 1837 by Heber C. Kimball. Heber later prophesied to Willard Richards, "Willard, I baptized your wife today." Although Willard and Jennetta had not yet seen each other, they soon met, fell in love and were married in England on September 24, 1838.

I married Jennetta…. Most truly do I praise my Heavenly Father for His great kindness in providing me a partner according to His promise. I receive her from the Lord, and hold her at His disposal. I pray that He may bless us forever. Amen! 30

Willard and Jennetta settled in Nauvoo and were blessed with a son, whom they named Heber John.

Jennetta became ill on May 21, 1845. On July 9, 1845, Willard wrote in his journal:

At day light dressed…[Jennetta] very weak…. I gave her encouragement as I felt. She said, "how can I die under such progress? About sunrise sent for Levi [Richards] [and] about 6 [A.M.] sent for Elder H. C. Kimball, who came and laid on hands and prayed, she revived. Also sent for Father John Smith, John Taylor, [and] George A. Smith. Heber Kimball, John E. Page, Levi Richards, and myself…went into her room anointed and prayed for her and felt encouraged. At fifteen minutes past 10 A.M., Jennetta stopped breathing. 31

ABOVE: *On March 26, 1845, in Nauvoo, a daguerreotype was taken of Willard Richards, his wife Jennetta and their son Heber John.* Image reproduced courtesy of Church Archives, The Church of Jesus Christ of Latter-day Saints and © Intellectual Reserve, Inc.
RIGHT: *On July 11, 1845, at the request of her young son, Jennetta was buried in the garden outside the Richards home, a sacred place, perhaps like this flowering garden on the road to Carthage. Her headstone is found close to the Richards' property just off Highway 96.*

In April, 1841, after serving in the English mission nearly four years, Willard returned and was appointed as Joseph's private secretary, Church recorder, clerk and historian. In November Joseph wrote in his journal, "I have been searching all my life to find a man after my own heart whom I could trust with my business in all things, and I have found him. Doctor Willard Richards is the man."[32]

In 1843, Joseph prophesied that "the time would come that the balls would fly around [Willard] like hail, and he should see his friends fall on the right and on the left, but that there should not be a hole in his garment."[33] This was fulfilled at Carthage.

When the jailer at Carthage asked Joseph to go into the cell to be safer, Joseph asked Willard if he would go with him. Willard said,

Bro. Joseph, you did not ask me to cross the river with you, you did not ask me to come to Carthage, you did not ask me to come to jail with you, and do you think I would forsake you now? But I will tell you what I will do, if you are condemned to be hung for treason, I will be hung in your stead and you shall go free. [34]

Willard was loyal to God and his friends throughout his life.

July 10, 1845
Sisters Durphy, Sessions, Rhonda Ann, Lucy Clayton, and Sister Wilcox dressed Jennetta and put her in her coffin about sunset. Heber [Richards] said, "Pa, will you bury Ma in the garden, if you do I can bear it. If you do not I cannot bear it." I told him I would bury her in the garden.

July 11, 1845
About sunset laid the coffin…in a vault in the S.W. corner of the door yard…. Threw a dahlia on the head of the coffin in the vault and said, "I will come and fetch it with her."[35]

_H_yrum, six years older than Joseph, took care of his little brother and supported him throughout his life. "One historian noted that Hyrum 'guarded his younger and more favored brother as tenderly as if the Prophet had been his son instead of his younger brother.' "36 While the family lived in Lebanon, New Hampshire, Joseph contracted typhus at age eight. Hyrum held Joseph's infected leg for three weeks to offer relief from pain. This loyalty continued in Nauvoo. Rachel Ivins Grant, mother of Heber J. Grant, said:

[O]f all the men she was acquainted with in her girlhood days in Nauvoo, she admired Hyrum Smith most for his absolute integrity and devotion to God, and his loyalty to the prophet of God. 37

Hyrum was one of the eight witnesses to the gold plates of The Book of Mormon, and at age 30 was the oldest of six men who organized the Church of Christ.

The Lord said of Hyrum Smith:

Blessed is my servant Hyrum Smith; for I, the Lord, love him because of the integrity of his heart and because he loveth that which is right before me. 38

Hyrum faithfully served as Acting President of the Church in Nauvoo while Joseph traveled to Washington, D.C. He was chairman of the Temple Building Committee, and was Presiding Patriarch

of the Church of Jesus Christ of Latter-day Saints.

Lucy, his mother, described him as "rather remarkable for his tenderness and sympathy." 39

He went through the trials and imprisonment Joseph suffered and acted "in concert" with him in all leadership capacities. 40

Joseph loved his brother Hyrum and said he had "the mildness of a lamb, and the integrity of a Job, and…the meekness and humility of Christ." 41

Hyrum had four children when his first wife, Jerusha, died. He married Mary Fielding and had two more children, a daughter and a son, Joseph F. Smith, who became the sixth President of the Church.

Mary's sense of humor in dealing with her new family and responsibilities was evident in a letter to her busy and out-of-town new husband; she ended her letter: "Your faithful companion and friend, but unhappy stepmother, Mary Smith." 42

Hyrum's grandson, Joseph Fielding Smith, became the tenth President of The Church of Jesus Christ of Latter-day Saints. He said of his grandfather:

No man was ever more closely associated with the Prophet than was the Patriarch Hyrum; no man understood the Prophet better. They were together through most of the trials and difficulties that beset the Saints. Together they shared joy and sorrow, and side by side they stood in their unjust imprisonments, persecutions, and sentence of death. 43

*T*he Prophet Joseph Smith was a significant part of the life of the city… the presiding elder and mayor…[he] was the main reason Nauvoo grew. Convert and curious came to him, and he welcomed them. For many of the Saints arriving in Nauvoo, this was their first opportunity to see a large gathering of Church members, and their first experience with the Prophet himself."[1]

Joseph wrote in his journal three days before Christmas, 1843:

At home at nine o'clock A.M. reading a magazine to my children. 2

Joseph had a sweet, young family consisting of Julia, 12 years, Joseph III, 11 years, Fredrick, 7 years, and Alexander, 5 years.

On January 6, 1842, Joseph opened the "Red Brick Store" in Nauvoo. Emma worked long and hard helping Joseph unload wagons full of supplies for the store, stocking the shelves and helping to run the store. On February sixth she gave birth to a son who did not live; this was the sixth baby's death that Emma and Joseph had endured. Only five months before, her fourteen-month-old baby, Don Carlos, had died from the effects of malaria. The Prophet Joseph and Emma Hale were the parents of eleven children (two children were adopted). Only four grew to adulthood.

The first child to survive was called Joseph after his father. He was born November 6, 1832, at

PREVIOUS PAGE LEFT: *Mary Fielding and Hyrum Smith.* Images courtesy of LDS Church Archives and © Intellectual Reserve, Inc.
PREVIOUS PAGE RIGHT: *Joseph and Emma greet their neighbors while on a stroll outside their home, the Homestead.* LEFT: *Joseph reads to his children inside the Homestead.* ABOVE LEFT: *Painting of the striking Emma Smith.* ABOVE: *Emma spent many hours waiting on customers in the Red Brick Store.*

Kirtland, Ohio. He was only eleven at the time of his father's death. In 1860, he became the President of the Reorganized Church, holding that position until his death, on December 10, 1914.

Emma cared for her mother-in-law, Lucy Mack Smith, until Lucy died in 1856. The Prophet's mother had always admired Emma and said of her:

I have never seen a woman in my life, who would endure every species of fatigue and hardship, from month to month, and from year to year with that unflinching courage, zeal, and patience, which she has ever done. 3

In Nauvoo Emma finally had a home of her own, a two-story log house named the Homestead.

But because of the constant flow of visitors from throughout the world, a larger home, called the Mansion House, was built in 1842 on a corner lot across from the Homestead. Eventually the Mansion House had twenty-two rooms; the Prophet's family occupied three and the rest served as hotel rooms. W.W. Phelps once remarked that Joseph, like the famous Napoleon, should have a smaller table in order to limit the number of guests inundating them. Emma's reply was, "Joseph is a bigger man than Napoleon; he could never eat without his friends."[4]

Emma's kindness and hospitality were legendary in Nauvoo. Jane Elizabeth Manning, a free black woman, walked with her children to Nauvoo to meet the prophet and gather with the Saints. "I was certain he was a prophet because… I saw him in Old Connecticut in a vision, saw him plain and knew he was a prophet." Her family was invited to "stay at the Mansion House until they found work and other accommodations."[5] Jane stayed at the Prophet's home, to help Emma care for the guests at the Mansion House.

"When George Q. Cannon arrived as a young English convert at the dock landing at Nauvoo, '…large numbers crowded…to welcome the emigrants…. [I] sought with a boy's curiosity and

LEFT: *Joseph and Emma receiving friends at the Mansion House.* ABOVE: *The Mansion House in the summer.*

eagerness…to get sight of the Prophet…whom [I had] never met. When [my] eyes fell upon the Prophet…[I] knew him instantly.' "[6]

Emma and Joseph gave up their bed often and slept on the floor with coats thrown over them. Lucy Mack Smith records:

How often I have parted every bed in the house for the accommodation of the brethren, and then laid a single blanket on the floor for my husband and myself, while Joseph and Emma slept upon the same floor, with nothing but their cloaks for both bed and bedding.[7]

Emmeline B. Wells said of Emma:

Sister Emma was benevolent and hospitable; she drew around her a large circle of friends, who were like good comrades. She was motherly in nature to young people, always had a houseful to entertain or be entertained. She was very high-spirited, and the brethren and sisters paid her great respect. Emma was a great solace to her husband in all his persecutions and the severe ordeals through which he passed; she was always ready to encourage and comfort him, devoted to his interests, and was constantly by him whenever it was possible. She was queen in her home, so to speak, and beloved by the people, who were many of them indebted to her for favors and kindnesses.[8]

The following story sheds wonderful insight into the kind of man Joseph Smith was:

After arriving in Nauvoo we were five or six weeks looking for employment, but failed to get any. One morning I said to my brother-in-law, "Let us go and see the Prophet. I feel that he will give us something to do."…[We] found him in a little store selling a lady some goods. This was the first time I had had an opportunity to be near him and get a good look at him. I felt there was a superior spirit in him. He was different to anyone I had ever met before; and I said in my heart, he is truly a Prophet of the most high God.

As I was not a member of the Church I wanted Henry to ask him for work, but he did not do so, so I had to. I said, "Mr. Smith, if you please, have you any employment you could give us both, so we can get some provisions?"

He viewed us with a cheerful countenance, and with such a feeling of kindness said: "Well, boys, what can you do?"

We told him what our employment was before we left our native land.

Said he, "Can you make a ditch?"

I replied we would do the best we could at it.

"That's right, boys," and picking up a tape line he said, "Come along with me."

He took us a few rods from the store, gave me the ring to hold, and stretched all the tape from the reel and marked a line for us to work by.

"Now, boys," said he, "can you make a ditch

ABOVE: *The exterior of the Red Brick Store in winter.* RIGHT: *Portrayal of Joseph Smith and the boys in need inside the Red Brick Store.*

Both photographs taken with permission of the Community of Christ, World Headquarters, Independence, Missouri

three feet wide and two and a half deep along this line?"

We said we would do our best, and he left us. We went to work, and when it was finished I went and told him it was done.

He came and looked at it and said, "Boys, if I had done it myself it could not have been done better. Now come with me."

He led the way back to the store, and told us to pick the best ham or piece of pork for ourselves. Being rather bashful, I said we would rather he

would give us some. So he picked two of the largest and best pieces of meat and a sack of flour for each of us, and asked us if that would do. We told him we would be willing to do more work for it, but he said, "If you are satisfied, boys, I am."

We thanked him kindly, and went on our way home rejoicing in the kindheartedness of the Prophet of our God."[9]   —Elder James Leech

Joseph surprised strangers who supposed that a prophet would be sober and sedate, perhaps old and bearded. He had many attractive personal qualities, standing an athletic six feet tall, being robust and outgoing and fond of sports. It was said that nobody could best him at stick pulling or jumping the mark. In fact, his happy nature disgruntled some people.

One day two ministers visited him, trying to corner him in scriptural matters. Unbeaten there, Joseph walked outside, drew a mark on the ground, and jumped. Then he told the ministers that they hadn't bested him at the scriptures, so they might see if they could best him at jumping. They refused, walking away in disgust.[10]

…Joseph was studying Greek and Latin, and when he got tired studying he would go and play with the children in their games about the house, to give himself exercise. Then he would go back to his studies as before. I was a boy then about fourteen years old. He used to take me up on his knee and caress me as he would a child.

I relate this to show the kindness and simplicity of his nature. I never saw another man like Joseph. There was something heavenly and angelic in his looks that I never witnessed in the countenance of any other person. During his short stay I became very much attached to him, and learned to love him more dearly than any other person I ever met, my father and mother not excepted. 11   —Elder John W. Hess

Both photographs taken with permission of the Community of Christ, World Headquarters, Independence, Missouri

LEFT: *A depiction of Joseph stick pulling with several boys on the grass in front of the Homestead.*
ABOVE: *A depiction of John Hess sitting on the lap of his beloved friend, the Prophet, in the Red Brick Store.*

restling was a popular sport in Nauvoo, and Joseph Smith was very athletic, six feet tall and two hundred pounds. He was a champion wrestler.

The Prophet met Howard Coray, a schoolteacher, in April of 1839, a few months after Coray's baptism. Joseph hired Coray on the spot as his clerk.

One evening in a playful mood, the Prophet jokingly said, "Brother Coray, I wish you were a little larger. I would like to have some fun with you." Disregarding an arm crippled since birth and the seventy pounds Joseph Smith outweighed him by, Howard was eager for the challenge—and ended up with a broken leg.

The Prophet, smitten by remorse, watched over his convalescence anxiously and, when asked for a blessing, promised Howard, "You will soon find a companion, one that will be suited to your condition, and whom you will be satisfied with. She will cling to you, like the cords of death; and you will have a good many children."[12]

A few weeks later, Howard remembered the Prophet's blessing as he attended conference.

"My eyes settled upon a young lady, sitting in a one horse buggy…. She had dark brown eyes, very bright and penetrating; at least they penetrated me; and I said to myself, she will do; the fact is, I was decidedly struck." we…then fell into familiar conversation.

"This interview, though short, was indeed very enjoyable; and closed with the hope that she might

ABOVE: *One of Nauvoo's ten bishops, Joseph B. Noble and his family built this home in 1843. Lucy Mack Smith moved to the Noble Home on April 11, 1846, but lived there only a few months.* RIGHT: *A depiction of Joseph Smith and his beloved horse Joe Duncan. Photo taken close to the Hyrum Smith Farm.*

be the one whom the Lord had picked for me; and thus it proved to be."[13]

Howard Coray married Martha Jane Knowlton, and they were very happy. Martha bore thirteen children; twelve grew to adulthood.

Lucy Mack Smith would later dictate the history of her son, Joseph, to Martha Jane in 1845.

In 1842 the election for governor of Illinois was held. A candidate, Joseph Duncan, pledged that if elected, he would ride Joe Smith and the Mormons out of town. Joseph Smith had a sorrel horse whom he named "Joe Duncan." It gave Joseph some satisfaction to "ride Joe Duncan out of town" whenever he had a mind to.14

"*I am your friend and brother, and I wish to do you good.... The Great Spirit has given me a book, and told me that you will soon be blessed again. The Great Spirit will soon begin to talk with you and your children. This is the book which your fathers made. I wrote upon it. [He showed them the Book of Mormon and went on.] This tells what you will have to do. I now want you to begin to pray to the Great Spirit. ...Ask the Great Spirit for what you want, and it will not be long before the Great Spirit will bless you, and you will cultivate the earth and build good houses.... We will give you something to eat and to take home with you.*" An ox was killed for the Indians, who were also given more horses, and "*they went home satisfied and contented.*"15

—Joseph Smith

*I*n the autumn of 1841, Indian Chiefs Keokuk, Kiskukosh and Appenoose lead a caravan of about one hundred Sac and Fox braves and their families to Nauvoo to receive the Prophet's advice and benediction. Wilford Woodruff's journal records, "The Indian orator arose and said—

'We as a people have long been distressed and oppressed. We have been driven from our lands many times. We have been wasted away by wars, until there are but few of us left…. The Great Spirit has told us that he had raised up a great Prophet, chief, and friend, who would do us great good and tell us what to do; and the Great Spirit has told us that you are the man [here the speaker pointed to the Prophet Joseph Smith]. We have now come a great way to see you, and hear your words, and to have you tell us what to do. Our horses have become poor traveling and we are hungry. We will now wait and hear your words.'"[16]

The Spirit of God rested upon the Indian group, especially the orator. Joseph became greatly affected and wept.

My older brother and I were going to school, near the building which was known as Joseph's store. It had been raining the previous day, causing the ground to be very muddy, especially along that street. My brother Wallace and I both got fast in the mud and could not get out, and of course, childlike, we began to cry, for we thought we would have to stay there. But looking up, I beheld the loving friend of children, the Prophet Joseph, coming to us. He soon had us on higher and drier ground. Then he stooped down and cleaned the mud from our…shoes…and wiped our tear-stained faces. He spoke kind and cheering words to us, and sent us on our way to school rejoicing.[17]

—Margarette McIntire Burgess

PREVIOUS PAGE LEFT: *Depicted in this photo, left to right, are Blackhawk's son, Kiskukosh with a headdress roach of porcupine quills, identifying him of the war clan; Chief Keokuk with his staff of authority and peace pipe; two of Keokuk's wives in the background; Joseph Smith and Appenoose, the spiritual chief.* Photo taken courtesy of Nauvoo State Park. PREVIOUS PAGE RIGHT: *Depiction of Joseph comforting the children in front of the Red Brick Store.* ABOVE: *The Prophet Joseph practices speaking.* RIGHT: *Joseph preaches in the Grove.*

Not a single church meetinghouse was built in Nauvoo. Every Sunday morning at ten, weather permitting, Saints from throughout the city and nearby communities would gather in the "Grove" to hear the prophet, or one of the apostles, speak. Most descriptions refer to it as west of the temple but "on the temple site."

"It being in the open air, and the audience so large, it was with great difficulty he [Joseph Smith] could be heard by all present."[18]

Speaking to large groups in the great outdoors took a toll on one's voice and energy. They had no devices to carry their voice. Prompted by the clamor of horses, oxen, irreverent children, flirting teens and gossipy women, Heber C. Kimball stated that, the thought of speaking there gave him much pain.[19]

Joseph mentions in his journal, "After preaching, I gave some instruction about order in the congregation, men among women, and women among men, horses in the assembly, and men and boys on the stand who do not belong there, [etc.]"

James J. Monroe, who tutored Joseph's children, stated in his diary that he arose at 4:45 A.M.:

…and accompanied by Joseph proceeded to my usual place of morning retreat. On our way we met Oliver [Cowdery] who went with us. On our arrival we commenced our exercises, vis: hallowing, screaming, singing and speaking. [20]

The prophet constantly sought to improve himself, but Brigham Young said the following of his best friend of twelve years:

When I first heard him preach, he brought heaven and earth together; and all the priests of the day could not tell me anything correct about heaven, hell, God, angels or devils; they were as blind as Egyptian darkness. When I saw Joseph Smith, he took heaven, figuratively speaking, and brought it down to earth; and he took the earth, brought it up, and opened up, in plainness and simplicity, the things of God; and that is the beauty of his mission. [21]

I feel like shouting Hallelujah all the time, when I think that I ever knew Joseph Smith, the Prophet whom the Lord raised up and ordained, and to whom he gave keys and power to build up the kingdom of God on earth and sustain it. [22]

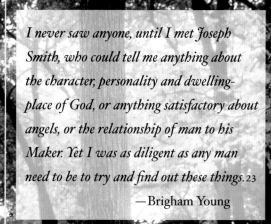

*I never saw anyone, until I met Joseph Smith, who could tell me anything about the character, personality and dwelling-place of God, or anything satisfactory about angels, or the relationship of man to his Maker. Yet I was as diligent as any man need to be to try and find out these things.*23

—Brigham Young

Those who lived and walked with the Prophet Joseph Smith made the following observations:

My first impressions were that he was an extra-ordinary man—a man of great penetration; was different from any other man I ever saw; had the most heavenly countenance, was genial, affable and kind, and looked the soul of honor and integrity. [24]   —Bathsheba W. Smith

I was favorably impressed with his noble mien [presence], his stately form and his pleasant, smiling face and cheerful conversation. [25]
—James Worthington Phippen

Brigham Young understood Joseph's problems being president and prophet, as well as businessman to support his family. Of the Saints that frequented Joseph's store, Brigham said:

Joseph was a first-rate fellow with them all the time, provided he never would ask them to pay him.... When he had let many of the brethren and sisters have goods on trust, he could not meet his liabilities, and then they would turn round and say, "What is the matter, brother Joseph, why don't you pay your debts? It is quite a curiosity that you don't pay your debts; you must be a bad financier, you don't know how to handle the things of the world." [26]

Both photographs taken with permission of the Community of Christ, World Headquarters, Independence, Missouri

ABOVE: Joseph and his son, Fredrick, look out a window at the Homestead. RIGHT: Joseph and Emma by the well at the Homestead.

Emma and Joseph loved each other dearly. "When Joseph was forced to leave Nauvoo to avoid arrest, she managed to join him after dark at an island on the Mississippi River." He later wrote,

With what unspeakable delight, and transports of joy swelled my bosom, when I took by the hand,…my beloved Emma—she that was my wife, even the wife of my youth, the choice of my heart. Many were the reverberations of my mind when I contemplated for a moment the many scenes we had been called to pass through, the fatigues and the toils, the sorrows and sufferings, and the joys and consolations, from time to time, which had strewed our paths and crowned our board. Oh what a commingling of thought filled my mind…, again she is here, even in the seventh trouble— undaunted, firm, and unwavering—unchangeable, affectionate Emma.27

Emma, with many other Saints, chose not to go west.

You may think I was not a very good Saint not to go West, but I had a home here and did not go because I did not know what I should have there.28

Emma, saint that she was, continued to care for others, leaving a legacy of selfless charity to Nauvoo.

Brigham Young said of the Prophet Joseph:

Though I admitted in my feelings and knew all the time that Joseph was a human being subject to err, still it was none of my business to look after his faults…. It was not for me to question whether Joseph was dictated by the Lord at all times and under all circumstances or not…. He was called of God; and if He had a mind to leave him to himself and let him commit an error, that was no business of mine. [Joseph Smith] was God's servant, and not mine. 29

ABOVE: *Joseph Smith prays in a secluded spot near his brother Hyrum's farm.* RIGHT: *A view of the Mississippi at sunset.*

LOSING A BELOVED PROPHET

*J*oseph's martyrdom was suggested while he was translating the Book of Mormon in March, 1829. The Lord promised him eternal life if he was "firm in keeping the commandments...even if you should be slain."1 On June 28, 1844, on viewing the bodies of her two oldest sons, Lucy said,

As I looked upon their peaceful, smiling countenances, I seemed almost to hear them say—"Mother, weep not for us, we have overcome the world by love; we carried to them the gospel, that their souls might be saved; they slew us for our testimony, and thus placed us beyond their power; their ascendancy is for a moment, ours is an eternal triumph."

*I then thought upon the promise which I had received in Missouri, that in five years Joseph should have power over all his enemies. The time had elapsed and the promise was fulfilled.*2

ABOVE: *Hyrum warns his brother Joseph of trouble as they stand on the bank of the Mississippi.*

On March 23, 1844, Joseph was told about a plot to kill the Smith family. Dennison L. Harris and Robert Scott, both seventeen, were invited to a secret meeting. The two boys asked Dennison's father, Emer, a brother to Martin Harris, what they should do. He contacted Joseph, who asked the boys to go and report back. More meetings were scheduled and attended. Before the fourth meeting Joseph told them, "This will be your last. Make no covenants, or enter into any obligations whatever with them." The boys were asked to take an oath for the destruction of Joseph. As they tried to leave they were taken to a cellar among drawn swords, bowie knives, cocked muskets and bayonets and again asked to take the oath. When they refused a sword was drawn over their heads. Someone shouted, "Hold on, the boys' parents very likely know where they are." They were told, "If you ever open your mouths concerning anything you have seen or heard…we will kill you…."[3] The boys were then escorted away. "They immediately took their course toward the river in the opposite direction from their homes, conveying to their enemies by word and act, that they would keep their secret. On the river bank they met the Prophet and an elder brother of Robert Scott, and to them they told their story."[4] Their bravery and loyalty brought the Prophet to tears.

The enemies against Nauvoo understood the strength of the Nauvoo Charter, a document which Joseph had presented and which had been passed by the Illinois legislature. The charter was a protection from mobs, illegal court proceedings and the whims of higher governmental agencies. Only the repeal of the charter by the state legislature could curtail these powers.

Conspirators at Nauvoo procured a press and proposed the publishing of a paper to be called the *Nauvoo Expositor*. The object of the paper, as set forth in the prospectus, was to advocate "the unconditional repeal of the Nauvoo City Charter, to restrain and correct the abuses of the 'unit power.'" On June 7, 1844, the first and only issue of the *Expositor* appeared "filled with...slanders against the Prophet and the leading citizens of Nauvoo,...attacking the charter."5

The city council held a meeting on June 10, where "the *Expositor* was declared a public nuisance and was ordered to be abated. The city marshal, John P. Greene, was instructed to proceed to the printing office and carry out the order of the council." He and a few men demanded entrance into the building, but were denied. Nevertheless, he opened the door, jumbled the type, took the press and set fire to the printed papers he found. He reported all this to the mayor who sent a description of the events to

ABOVE: *An exact replica of the* Nauvoo Expositor.

the governor of Illinois.

Enraged, "the conspirators set fire to the building and hastened to Carthage, stating that their lives were in danger and they had been driven from their homes. The fire was...extinguished before any damage had been done to the building, but the falsehoods circulated aroused the people of Carthage and other towns."6

The mobs had the cause they had been looking for to repeal the city charter and arrest Joseph.

On Sunday, May 26, 1844, a month before his death, Joseph addressed the Saints:

I, like Paul, have been in perils, and oftener than anyone in this generation.... I should be like a fish out of water, if I were out of persecutions. Perhaps my brethren think it requires all this to keep me humble. The Lord had constituted me so curiously that I glory in persecution. I am not nearly so humble as if I were not persecuted. When facts are proved, truth and innocence will prevail at last. My enemies are no philosophers. They think that when they have my spoke under, they will keep me down, but for the fools, I will hold on and fly over them. 7

On June 16, Joseph wrote to Governor Ford, calling his attention to mob meetings at Carthage and Warsaw and the threats made to exterminate the Saints. He requested the governor come to Nauvoo to make further investigation. The governor went to Carthage and sent a letter demanding that Joseph go to Carthage; he would guarantee Joseph's safety. A letter was sent to Brigham Young and the apostles on missions, telling them to return to Nauvoo at once.

On June 22, in the evening, Joseph soberly counseled with Hyrum and friends. Joseph's countenance brightened as he said,

The way is open. It is clear to my mind what to do. All they want is Hyrum and myself; then

Photographed with permission of the Community of Christ, World Headquarters, Independence, Missouri

ABOVE: *Depiction of a somber Joseph Smith at the Homestead.* RIGHT: *Orrin Porter Rockwell, the Prophet Joseph, his brother Hyrum, and Willard Richards preparing to flee across the Mississippi.*

tell everybody to go about their business.... There is no doubt they will come here and search for us. Let them search; they will not harm you in person or property, and not even a hair of your head. We will cross the river tonight, and go away to the West. 8

Joseph wrote in his journal:

I told Stephen Markham that if Hyrum and I were ever taken again we should be massacred, or I was not a prophet of God. 9

About midnight, Orrin P. Rockwell rowed Joseph, Hyrum and Willard Richards across the river with the order to return with supplies and horses to begin the trip to the Rocky Mountains the next day. At ten o'clock A.M., a posse arrived in Nauvoo to arrest the Prophet. At one o'clock P.M., Rockwell and Reynolds Cahoon returned with a letter from Emma and word from Hiram Kimball and Lorenzo Wasson. Hiram and Lorenzo accused Joseph of cowardice saying that their property would be destroyed and they would be left without house or home. Joseph replied, "If my life is of no value to my friends, it is of none to myself." Hyrum decided they should return. The Prophet remained in deep reflection for some time and said, "If you go back I will go with you, but we shall be butchered." While walking to the river Joseph fell behind. The others shouted for him to hurry. Joseph replied, "It is of no use to hurry, for we are going back to be slaughtered."10

On the morning of June 24, 1844, Joseph bid another farewell to his family, knowing this would be the last time he would see them. Then, on this hot, humid day, the large contingency of men began the 26½ mile journey to Carthage. Joseph stopped as they passed his farm and looked a good while. As they continued on, he kept looking back; he could also see the temple in the distance,

> If some of you had such a farm, and knew you would not see it any more, you would want to take a good look at it for the last time. 11

"Greater love hath no man than that he should lay down his life for his friends." You have stood by me in the hour of trouble, and I am willing to sacrifice my life for your preservation.[12]

—Joseph Smith, June 18, 1844

FAR LEFT: *Trail to the Pioneer Burial Grounds.* TOP LEFT: *On the Martyrdom Trail.* BELOW LEFT: *A field of corn grows close to the Sarah Granger Kimball Home.* ABOVE: *A view of the Seventies Hall from Granger Street.*

*J*oseph was incarcerated in the Carthage jail, accompanied by his brother Hyrum, John Taylor, Willard Richards, John S. Fullmer and Dan Jones.

*It was late at night when the prisoners tried to get some rest. At first Joseph and Hyrum occupied the only bed in the jail room, but a gunshot during the night and a disturbance led Joseph's friends to insist that he take a place between the two of them on the floor. They would protect him with their own bodies.*13

The next day all but two of Joseph's friends were made to leave the prison. John Taylor sang "A Poor Wayfaring Man of Grief" two times at the prophet's request.

Soon after, men with painted faces rushed the stairs and shot Hyrum through the door and killed him. Joseph went to the window to draw fire off the others. He was shot, killed and fell outside to the ground. John Taylor, shot four times, was severely wounded. Dr. Richards, unhurt, went for help after carrying John Taylor into the other room and covering him with a mattress.

On June 28, 1844, at eight A.M., Dr. Willard Richards arrived in Nauvoo with the bodies of Joseph and Hyrum on two wagons, accompanied by their brother Samuel H. Smith.

ABOVE: *The jail at Carthage, Illinois. The Prophet Joseph fell from the top floor window seen in the shadows at right. The mob awaited him below.* RIGHT: *The Ashby/Snow duplex.*

I sat upon the steps of my father's house on the evening of the day that [Joseph] was shot until twelve o'clock and never did I hear before such an uproar and noise that seemed to pervade the very atmosphere; dogs howling, mingled with confused noises as though all the legions of the damned were in commotion.

Not dreaming of the tragedy that had been enacted that afternoon, I went to bed, but at dawn of morning the sad tale was brought to our ears and the grief and sorrow of a whole people cannot be pictured in language; for days, a man, woman or child could not be met but they were in tears for the loss of their beloved leader.

Soon the wagons containing the two brothers arrived in the city and passed down to the Mansion House where we visited and viewed their marred features as they lay in the hallowments of the grave.

Brother Willard Richards was the only one of the Twelve Apostles who was in Nauvoo. John Taylor being wounded, remained in Carthage. Soon the Twelve began to return, also Sidney Ridgon, who endeavored to have himself elected as guardian of the Church. 14

—Benjamin Ashby, 16 years old

"While the wagons carrying the bodies were still a long way off, the entire population of Nauvoo went out to meet them. No greater tribute could be paid than was paid that day to Joseph and Hyrum Smith. …Once when Joseph had been asked how he had acquired so many followers and retained them, he replied, 'It is because I possess the principle of love. All I can offer the world is a good heart and a good hand.'"16

Louisa Pratt remembered:

I rushed into my garden when the news was confirmed and poured out my soul…. I could feel no anger or resentment. I felt the deepest humility before God. I thought continually of his words "Be still and know that I am God."…Had Joseph given the command, every man, woman, and child would have stood to his defense, even to the loss of their own lives. 17

Joseph and Hyrum were taken to the Mansion House. On June 29TH, they were interred amidst the deep mourning of a stricken people. Before the funeral, about ten thousand Saints viewed the bodies at the Mansion House. Afterwards, two decoy coffins were filled with sand and buried. At about midnight the coffins containing the bodies were buried secretly in the basement of the unfinished Nauvoo House. Their bodies were reburied later in the Smith family plot.

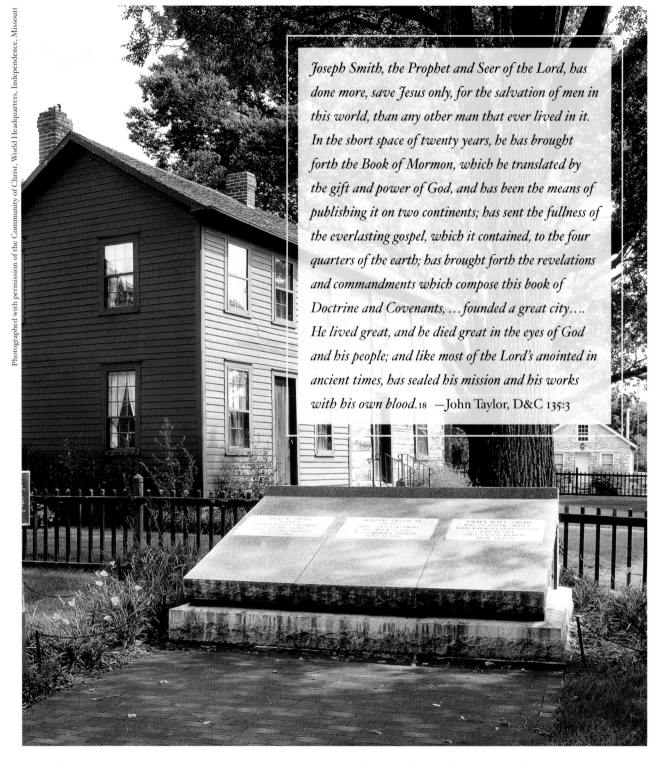

Photographed with permission of the Community of Christ, World Headquarters, Independence, Missouri

Joseph Smith, the Prophet and Seer of the Lord, has done more, save Jesus only, for the salvation of men in this world, than any other man that ever lived in it. In the short space of twenty years, he has brought forth the Book of Mormon, which he translated by the gift and power of God, and has been the means of publishing it on two continents; has sent the fullness of the everlasting gospel, which it contained, to the four quarters of the earth; has brought forth the revelations and commandments which compose this book of Doctrine and Covenants, …founded a great city…. He lived great, and he died great in the eyes of God and his people; and like most of the Lord's anointed in ancient times, has sealed his mission and his works with his own blood. 18 —John Taylor, D&C 135:3

ABOVE: *Hyrum, Emma and Joseph are buried outside the Homestead.* RIGHT: *Joseph and Hyrum Smith statue at Carthage.*

I do not regard my own life. I am ready to be offered a sacrifice for this people; for what can our enemies do? Only kill the body, and their power is then at an end. Stand firm, my friends; never flinch. Do not seek to save your lives, for he that is afraid to die for the truth, will lose eternal life…. God has tried you. You are a good people; therefore I love you with all my heart. [19]
—Joseph Smith

Joseph begged Hyrum not to go to Carthage with him. According to a blessing given to Hyrum in 1835 by the First Presidency, he was promised "power to escape his enemies *if he chose:*" [20]

Thou shalt have power to escape the hand of thine enemies. Thy life shall be sought with untiring zeal, but thou shalt escape. If it please thee, and thou desirest, thou shalt have the power voluntarily to lay down thy life to glorify God. [21]

I had been abused and thrust into a dungeon, and confined for months on account of my faith, and the "testimony of Jesus Christ." However I thank God that I felt a determination to die, rather than deny the things which my eyes had seen, which my hand had handled, and which I had borne testimony to…. [22] —Hyrum Smith

*I spent the day in the council with the Twelve Apostles at the house of President [Brigham] Young, conversing with them upon a variety of subjects. Brother Joseph Fielding was present, having been absent four years on a mission to England. I told the brethren that the Book of Mormon was the most correct of any book on earth, and the keystone of our religion, and a man would get nearer to God by abiding by its precepts, than by any other book.*23

—Joseph Smith, November 28, 1841

ABOVE: *Many important decisions concerning the future of the Saints were made in this room within Brigham Young's home.* RIGHT: *A depiction of a worker finishing the original Nauvoo Temple.*

We labored ten hours a day, and got something to take to our families for supper and breakfast. Many times we got nothing; at other times we got a half pound of butter or three pounds of fish, beef, and nothing to cook it with. Sometimes we got a peck of cornmeal or a few records of flour…or anything we could get to sustain us…and thank God that I and my family were thus blessed…. I have seen those that cut stone by the year eat nothing but parched or browned corn for breakfast and take some in their pockets for their dinner and go to work singing the songs of Zion. I mention this not to find fault or to complain, but to let my children know how the temple of Nauvoo was built, and how their parents as well as hundreds of others suffered to lay a foundation on which they could build and be accepted of God…. We would rather live poor and keep the commandments of God in building a temple than to live better and be rejected with our dead."1

— Luman Shurtliff

As a young woman, Sarah Granger Kimball attended the School of the Prophets with her father, Oliver Granger, in Kirtland. When she was older, she often mentioned her school experiences to underscore the importance she placed upon doctrinal study and education among women. 2 She was a leader in the community and desired to assist all she could in building the temple. Sarah's husband, Hiram, lived in Commerce prior to the Saints settling there and renaming it Nauvoo. He owned considerable property but was not a member of the Church. As Hiram was admiring their newborn son, she asked, "Is he worth $1,000?" Hiram replied he was worth at least that much.

FAR LEFT: *A chalk portrait of Sarah Granger Kimball.* LEFT: *A depiction of Sarah Kimball holding her newborn son in her home.* ABOVE: *Sarah and Hiram Kimball's home was originally built before the Saints arrived in Nauvoo and before brickyards were constructed. This explains the Kimball home being of frame construction, similar to homes in New England, where Hiram was from, rather than of brick. The reconstruction of the Kimball home was funded by the LDS Relief Society organization.*

ABOVE: The Kimball family Bible is one of the only personal effects found in Sarah and Hiram's home today. It is open to the book of Job. RIGHT: This rare plate commemorates the organization of the Relief Society in 1842. Photo courtesy of Museum of Church History and Art and © Intellectual Reserve, Inc.

Sarah said she was "donating her half-interest in their son as tithing for the temple. Hiram told the Prophet of the incident, who joked, "I accept all such donations, and from this day the boy shall stand recorded, church property." When Joseph suggested Hiram donate 500 dollars and retain possession, Hiram asked if city property was an acceptable substitute. Being told it was, he promptly donated an entire city block to the Church. 3

The organization of the Relief Society came directly from Sarah Granger Kimball's and Miss Cook's (Sarah's seamstress) desire to relieve the men's dire need of clothing while working on the temple. Some who worked on the temple wore no shoes or shirts. 4

Charles Lambert arrived in Nauvoo as a new convert and applied for work on the temple. He was told there was plenty of work, but no pay at the present time. Having no working clothes, he reported for work in what he had worn as a contractor in England—a fine suit and high silk hat. He put on an apron and went to work.

Sarah Kimball and Miss Cook worked out a plan to make shirts for workers. Sarah would donate cloth and Miss Cook would sew them. They desired to begin an organization to involve friends and others who wanted to help. Eliza R. Snow was asked to draw up by-laws for their organization and Joseph Smith was asked to look them over.

The Prophet Joseph Smith organized the Female Relief Society in the upper room of the Red Brick Store on Thursday afternoon, March 17, 1842, with a membership of eighteen. Thirty-seven-year-old Emma Smith was chosen as president, with Emma's dear friend, Sarah M. Cleveland, as a counselor. Sarah had significantly demonstrated her charity through housing Emma, her family and the Rigdon family after their Missouri exodus into

Quincy, Illinois. Elizabeth Ann Whitney, Bishop Newel K. Whitney's wife, was another counselor and Eliza R. Snow, secretary.

"[Emma's] was not a token presidency because she was the wife of the Prophet; she was a strong, independent woman in her own right."5

*On 28 April [1842] the Prophet gave the sisters additional counsel and promises. He advised the women to treat their husbands "'with mildness and affection' and to meet them with a 'smile instead of an argument or a murmur,' reminding them that when a mind is in despair it needs the 'solace of affection and kindness.'"*6

At the second meeting, Lucy Mack Smith, the Prophet's mother, said,

*This institution is a good one…. We must cherish one another, watch over one another, comfort one another and gain instruction, that we may all sit down in heaven together.*7

ABOVE: Depiction of Joseph teaching the men working on the temple as they take a break for lunch.
RIGHT: This quarry, now under water, is very close to where the stone from the original temple was cut.

Joseph Smith labored alongside his people on the temple. Young, and strong, he enjoyed physical exertion and was happy to work. While working, he could often be found teaching the people as the Savior did. A frequent plea was, "Brother Joseph, talk to us." "I could lean back and listen. Ah what pleasure this would give me," wrote Wandle Mace. 8

During these gospel conversations, Joseph explained the covenants made and ordinances performed in holy temples. He taught that through receiving temple ordinances they would have power given to become more committed to a Christlike life and have greater love for God. Joseph taught, "The pleasing joys of family ties and associations contribute to the happiness, power and dominion of those who attain to the celestial glory." 9 He also promised that those who had worked so hard on the temple would be the first to receive their endowment: "[They] shall have the first claim to receive their endowments in the temple." 10

In September of 1843, Emma Smith was the first woman to receive this blessing. The ordinance was performed in the upstairs room of the Mansion House. Following this, "she then presided over the administration of the temple ordinances for the women." 11

By 1842, at least one hundred men worked just in the quarries, drilling and blasting tons of rock down, hewing it into two-ton blocks and loading it on specially made ox carts to the temple stone shop. More than one hundred casks of blasting powder were used at the quarry. Ten to twenty teams of oxen and wagons were employed each day. Joseph was often found assisting wherever there was a need, even extricating wagons and animals from the notorious Nauvoo mud.

Charles Lambert worked on the temple by day and stood watch protecting it against mob destruction by night. His commitment to finishing the temple was evidenced by this promise: "I would stick to the temple—pay or no pay until finished."

He came home one day to find his wife crying; she said she could bear anything but her children crying for bread when there was nothing to give them. The faithful parents prayed for help. "An hour later, Lucius Scovil came and asked Charles to make a gravestone to mark the spot where his fourteen-year-old son was buried. He had no money but would trade wheat—in advance." That very evening Lambert received four bushels of wheat from Brother Scovil. "Thus," Charles said, "was our prayer answered."12

ABOVE: The grave of 14-year-old Joel F. Scovil is found in the Pioneer Burial Grounds. RIGHT: The front of the Scovil Bakery. This home may have originally had two levels.

*I want the poor… to have a chance [to give]. The widow's two mites were more in the eyes of the Lord than the purse of the rich.*13

*M*ercy Fielding Robinson and her sister, Mary Fielding Smith began a "pennies for nails for the temple collection." The British Saints assisted these women, giving their energies to secure nails, windows, food, and clothing for the laborers. One sister, Drusilla Hendricks, even paid a good deal of tithing by making gloves and mittens.

Hyrum Smith, chairman of the Temple Building Committee, said:

The sisters resolved to pay fifty cents each towards buying nails and glass. By the utmost sacrifice, Louisa Pratt scraped together the amount. She was tempted by the needs of her family, but said:

*If I have no more than a crust of bread each day for a week, I will pay this money into the treasury. I went forward, paid over the money, and returned, feeling secret satisfaction.*14

ABOVE: *The home of William Weeks, architect for the original Nauvoo temple.*
RIGHT: *Charles Allen, craftsman for the new Nauvoo Temple windows, examines his work. There are 26 stained glass windows in the temple with 2,500 hand-split tapered joinery pegs used to construct the windows. No glue or nails were used.*

For the original Nauvoo temple, northern white pine from the pineries of Wisconsin was floated down the Mississippi to be used. Men were called on missions to the pineries. "The timber was floated down river, forming large rafts that covered nearly an acre and 'contained one hundred thousand feet of sawed lumber and sixteen thousand cubic feet, or one hundred ninety-two thousand square feet, of hewn lumber.' "15

Because this species of white pine has long since been used up in the sizes necessary for the temple reconstruction, sugar pine, a species of white pine that grows in northern California and southern Oregon was used. Charles Allen, craftsman for the new Nauvoo Temple, found a company that could provide the pine, but when he told the manager he might need about 12,000 board feet, the man responded, "Not on this planet! You'll be lucky to get 3,000."16 They obtained all 12,000 board feet.

William Weeks, architect for the original temple, met with the Prophet Joseph Smith for instruction and was told that circular windows would be needed to light the interior of the temple. Brother Weeks responded that round windows in the broad side of a building violated all known rules of architecture, and that they should be semi-circular. Joseph Smith responded:

I wish you to carry out my designs. I have seen in vision the splendid appearance of that building illuminated, and will have it built according to the pattern shown me. 16

Late in the evening…we came in sight of some neat cottages fenced with pickets, manifesting to us that the hand of industry was there different from anything we had seen since leaving England, even by the light of the moon; this was the first we saw of the city of the Saints…. We soon passed the temple, went from street to street, as in some large city…. I can truly say that the place, in general, exceeds my expectations. 18

—Joseph Fielding, upon returning
from a mission to the British Isles

With the death of Joseph and Hyrum, many thought that the work on the temple would be stopped. Five days after the martyrdom, the Saints reaffirmed their commitment to finish the temple and voted to resume work at once, even though they had no money to pay workers. Determination to complete the temple united the people. So many responded to calls for help that some workmen were assigned to other projects. "The sisters pledged to continue their 'penny contributions.'"[19]

The Saints prayed for the weather to hold so that the thirty pilasters, with moonstones at the bottom and sunstones at the top, could be finished before winter. The final capital was placed at noon on December 6, 1844, two hours before a brisk snowfall began. The Saints believed,

The Lord held up the storms and the cold for our advantage, until this important piece of labor had been accomplished.[20]

LEFT: *A view of the temple from the Browning Log Cabin.* ABOVE: *A temple builder depicts cleaning mortar from some bricks of the temple. During the completion of the exterior of the new Nauvoo Temple, Illinois experienced an unseasonably warm winter, with very little snow. Temperatures in January, 2002, were sometimes 60° F.* ABOVE RIGHT: *An antique hand drill.*

Wilford Woodruff recorded in his journal the Saints' necessity to finish the temple. "They felt that these ordinances would give to them a new spiritual life and that they would be better qualified in consequence as messengers of the word of God to the nations of the earth."21

Endowments began December 10, 1845. Heber C. Kimball was assigned the major responsibility of providing endowment ceremonies, and his personal journal became the official temple record.

Dozens of people received their endowments each day. On Christmas Day, 107 people received their endowment. Workers washed the white clothing each night so ordinance work could continue without interruption the following day.

PREVIOUS PAGE LEFT: *The reconstructed Nauvoo Temple at night.* PREVIOUS PAGE RIGHT: *A view of the temple from the Seventies Hall.* ABOVE: *A replica of the original Nauvoo Temple's Angel Moroni weathervane is found upstairs in the library of the Seventies Hall.*

The Nauvoo Temple has two intertwined olive branches around the steeple's clock. The olive tree was one of the symbols of the land of Israel.

The clock faces the cardinal points: East, West, North and South. Christ will come in the East and all flesh will see him.

The Angel Moroni of the first Nauvoo Temple was fashioned in a horizontal manner as a weather vane, as if to illustrate Revelation 14:6–7.

One of the angel's hands holds an open Book of Mormon, "which represents the restoration of the everlasting gospel in its purity. In the other hand he holds a trumpet to his lips. …When…living in England, the young John Taylor saw a vision of an angel 'flying through the midst of Heaven with a trumpet to his lips.' This vision is said to have been seen on the day that this heavenly messenger visited Joseph Smith and announced the existence of the Book of Mormon."[22]

The pattern for the original Nauvoo Temple was a three-story limestone building measuring 128 feet in length and 88 feet in width, with belfry, clock tower and weathervane. Its walls were three feet thick at ground level with some individual stones weighing as much as 4,000 pounds. Its tower and spire measured 158 feet above the ground. The tower of the restored temple is visible from a distance of twenty miles and can be seen over the trees on the road to Nauvoo from Keokuk, Iowa.

"In the ancient Israelite world, some thought of temples as places where heaven and earth met."[23] The exterior of the Nauvoo Temple with its light-colored limestone, stained-glass star windows, sunstones, moonstones and star stones is a symbol of heaven sitting comfortably on an elevated bluff, enjoying the view of her people, beckoning all to come. A sunstone with a human face gives multitudes of light rays as trumpets announce the arrival of the heavenly fortress repelling the forces of evil. Inside the fortress is found the power of Christ's love—"I am Messiah, the King of Zion, the Rock of Heaven, which is broad as eternity; whoso cometh in at the gate and climbeth up by me shall never fall."[24]

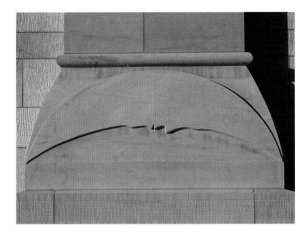

The order of architecture was unlike anything in existence, it was purely original, being a representation of the Church, the Bride, the Lamb's wife. John the Revela[tor], in the [twelvth] chapter, first verse says, "And there appeared a great wonder in heaven; a woman clothed with the sun, and the moon under her feet, and upon her head a crown of twelve stars." This is portrayed in the beautifully cut stone of this grand temple.[25]

— Wandle Mace, Original Nauvoo Temple Construction Foreman

"The architectural symbolism on the outside of the Nauvoo Temple indicated the nature of the ordinances that were performed within its walls."[26]

ABOVE LEFT: *A moonstone of the reconstructed Nauvoo Temple.* ABOVE: *There were 30 original sunstones, but only three are accounted for today. One stood outside the John Wood Mansion and Visitors' Center in Quincy, Illinois. John Wood was an early founder of Quincy and was extremely charitable to the Saints fleeing across the Mississippi River from the Missouri mobbings in the winter of 1838–39, and again when they fled from mob violence in Nauvoo in the winter of 1846. Note: While the original temple had walls of solid stone, here one can see the stone façade that adorns the thoroughly modern, reinforced concrete construction.*

*B*righam Young placed the capstone on the temple May 24, 1845. By August, the roof was finished, the building was enclosed, and work had begun on the tower. In England, the British Saints raised money to purchase a bell.

Brigham Young left Nauvoo on February 15, 1846, after giving at least 5,615 endowments, promising all Saints who weren't able to receive their endowments that there would be other temples in the West. The temple wasn't finished when Brigham left, but the Saints were determined that nothing would hinder them in their religious obligation of completing and dedicating the sacred temple. By April, the temple was given its final dedication and was soon abandoned.

At one time, Church leaders hoped to sell the Nauvoo Temple to the Catholic Church. No buyer was found and on the last day of April, in a special session directed by Wilford Woodruff and Orson Hyde, Joseph Young, Brigham's brother, delivered the building over to the Lord.

On October 9, 1848, fire broke out in the temple and quickly engulfed the entire structure; the fire may have been an act of vandalism. Then, in 1850, a tornado leveled part of the temple walls and weakened the rest. The stones became building materials for other buildings in the area, which can be seen today on Nauvoo's Mulholland Street.

ABOVE: This daguerreotype was taken in 1845 of the Nauvoo Temple. Image courtesy of International Society, Daughters of the Utah Pioneers.
RIGHT: The new Nauvoo Temple on a moonlit winter night in the final weeks of its reconstruction.

Every temple, be it large or small, old or new, is an expression of our testimony that life beyond the grave is as real and certain as is mortality. There would be no need for temples if the human spirit and soul were not eternal. Every ordinance performed in these sacred houses is everlasting in its consequences. 27

—President G. B. Hinckley, May 1993

President Gordon B. Hinckley's father, Bryant S. Hinckley, suggested consideration be given to the rebuilding of the Nauvoo temple. President Hinckley said:

I count it something of a strange and wonderful coincidence, that I've had a part in the determination of rebuilding this temple. 28

The new building will stand as a memorial to those who built the first structure. 29

—Gordon B. Hinckley

ABOVE: *A depiction of bringing a horse to be shod at the Webb Blacksmith Shop. This was done according to use of the horse; for a favorite horse ridden daily, perhaps quarterly. A wrangler on the reenacted Trek (1997) from Nauvoo to Salt Lake City shod his horse three times. Hooves are trimmed and new shoes nailed on to protect a horse's hoof from sharp rocks. Some blacksmiths carried a library of sized shoes and fitted them to the horse.*
RIGHT: *The back of the Webb Blacksmith Shop.*

*I*n February of 1844, Joseph Smith prophesied the Saints would settle in the Rocky Mountains. "I instructed the Twelve Apostles to send out a delegation and… hunt out a good location, where we can remove after the temple is completed."1

Still, he was proud of Nauvoo and prior to his death wrote: "Nauvoo continues to flourish, and the little one has become a thousand…. [There are] a number of splendid houses being erected and the Temple is rapidly progressing."2

This was the paradox of Nauvoo. The Saints knew they couldn't stay, but nourished their city as though they would never leave. They even transplanted chestnut trees as they left the city. In a similar way the Saints chose to transplant their families to a new desert home, where they could flourish.

On October 1, 1845, at John Taylor's home, the Twelve Apostles, led by Brigham Young, met with many people who were anxious for the Saints to leave Nauvoo. These included the commander of the Illinois state militia, General John J. Hardin, and Judge Stephen A. Douglas. They wanted "an action which would appease the mob and bring an end to the persecution, murders and house burning."[3]

Brigham told them they were not planting winter wheat and would leave in the spring as soon as "the grass grows and the water runs." He presented a plan of dividing the people into independent preparation companies of one hundred families. To further emphasize their plan to leave, Brigham sent a letter explaining:

> *one thousand families…compris[ing] from five to six thousand souls…are fully determined to remove in the spring, independent of the contingency of selling our property. We have some hundreds of farms, and some 2,000 or more houses for sale…and we request all good citizens to assist in the disposal of our property…. If all these testimonies are not sufficient to satisfy any people that we are in earnest, we will soon give them a sign that cannot be mistaken; we will leave them![4]*

ABOVE: *A wainwright built and repaired wagons. It took one man approximately one month to make one wagon. An ox-drawn wagon had no seat for a driver. Oxen were one-fourth the price of a horse, could pull more weight, feed on trail grass, and could be used for food if necessary.* RIGHT: *A close-up photograph of wagons in front of the Blacksmith Shop.* ABOVE RIGHT: *A bee catcher.*

> *The fall of 1845 found Nauvoo, as it were, one vast mechanic shop, as nearly every family was engaged in making wagons. Our parlor was used as a paint shop in which to paint wagons.*[5]
> —Bathsheba Smith

The Saints and their resources were stretched to the limit. They had a monumental temple to finish, temple clothes to make, and endowments and sealings to be done for 5,615 souls between December 10 and February 7. They needed to obtain and cure lumber and iron to make and cover wagons, which then needed to be packed and supplied with oxen, horses, cows, chickens, seeds and farm implements. Not only did missionaries need to be supported, but incoming converts needed to be housed, fellowshipped and readied for the journey. Maps, letters, papers and facts needed to be gathered for the *History of the Church* compilation. Explorers had to be interviewed and research done on the Western U.S. There were mobbing victims to be comforted, sustained and outfitted, and property and possessions to be sold. And, in addition to all of this, the Saints performed the day-to-day activities involved with childbirth, illness, death and survival.

How well I remember what a hard time [Father] had breaking in the animals to draw the wagon. There were six cows and two oxen. The oxen were well broken and quite sedate. But the cows were wild and unruly.... While Father was breaking the cattle, Mother was praying.... Many nights when we were in bed asleep... she would go out into the orchard... and there pour out her soul in prayer, asking the Lord to open the way for us to go with the Saints. 6 — Margaret Judd Clawson

LEFT: Depiction of the Clawson children preparing for the journey west with the Saints. Taken on the Hasek farm in Nauvoo.
ABOVE: A family prepares to cross the Mississippi at the end of the Trail of Hope.

*B*righam reassured his people:

> *Let there be no feelings about who shall go first;*
> *those who go first will lay a foundation for those*
> *who shall come after, and none will be neglected*
> *in their time. I have one request…that they be*
> *subject to their leaders, with their property and*
> *means and if this is done I can say there never*
> *will be a lack in the church…. I propose that*
> *all the Saints lay down their property to be used*
> *in building the Temple, the Nauvoo House and*
> *helping the poor away, such as must go in the*
> *first company.* 7

The first wagon to leave Nauvoo was that belonging to the Shumway family on February 4, 1846. The second wagon to leave Nauvoo belonged to Bishop George Miller and family, who crossed over the Mississippi on February 6, 1846. Other Saints began to leave earlier than planned as arrest warrants were issued for many of the apostles and leaders.

Bishop Miller had allowed himself to be captured outside the temple when the arrest was really for Brigham Young on a false charge of counterfeiting. Miller was taken two hours to Carthage and put in the Hamilton House Tavern (as Joseph Smith had been) before the mistake was discovered. The marshal was so angry he vowed revenge on Bishop Miller.

*M*y last act in that precious spot was to tidy
the rooms, sweep up the floor, and set the broom in
its accustomed place behind the door. Then with
emotions in my heart…. I gently closed the door
and faced an unknown future; faced it with faith
in God and with no less assurance of the ultimate
establishment of the Gospel in the West and of its
true, enduring principles, than I had felt in those
trying scenes in Missouri. 8   —Bathsheba Smith

Those whose lives were in imminent danger put together what they had and left in freezing February. Some Saints gave what they had prepared to those leaving early, as did Peter Conover, who said:

> *I had a wagon for my own use all ready for the cover when Brother Brigham came along and asked whose wagon it was. Someone told him it was mine. He came to me and told me that they had enough wagons, lacking one, to take the first company out. "Well," said I, "if you need that wagon, take it, and welcome." That left me without one, but I soon had another one ready.* 9

Erastus Snow recorded his departure:

> *I effected a sale of my household and personal property at a great sacrifice, gathered up what teams and provisions I could and started on the 16 of February... leaving my buildings and real estate at the disposal of Brothers Babbitt, Heywood, and Fullmer, the new trustees elected to remain and complete the lower stories of the Temple, attend to the sale of property, and wind up the affairs of the Church and from the proceeds to assist the poor in following us.* 10

LEFT: *Depiction of Bathsheba Smith inside the Lucy Mack Smith home.* RIGHT: *Depiction of Peter Conover giving his wagon to Brigham Young.*

Our way led through a prairie county and as we passed along I carried a heavy heart. I had now been a member of this Church nearly ten years and had been compelled to move my family four times and start anew. I had lived in Nauvoo the longest by half of any other place since I belonged to the Church. This place was endeared to me for the sweet association I had enjoyed with the Prophet, patriarch and the apostles of the most high. Here I was leaving the body of my dear wife and child, never to behold those places again in the flesh. I turned my back to the west and took a last look at the Nauvoo Temple and its surroundings and bade them good-bye forever. 11   —Luman Shurtliff

Despite the cold, almost every night, William Pitt's Brass Band would play music and many would dance. Around the campfires they sang songs like "Home Sweet Home." 12

Lorenzo Dow Young took his family across the river. His eight-year-old son, John, recalled this day:

In our home since early morning, all has been hurry and bustle; two wagons stand in our front yard, and my father with two other men, strangers to me, are carrying out our household goods. My mother looks pale, and when I ask her, "What is the matter?" she takes me in her arms, kisses me, and says, "We are going to leave our home, and will never see it again!" Just then some other teams come along, and one of the brethren calls to my father to be sure to put out the fire, and to hurry up, for it is getting late. In a few minutes mother and the children are lifted tenderly into the wagon. Father next takes his place on the front seat, turns his face to the west, and his back upon the home, which it had taken seven years of sacrifice and toil to build.

*At the river are three flatboats, or scows. Here and there on the banks of the river stand pale-faced mothers cuddling their little ones, while husbands and fathers quietly, yet resolutely, roll the wagons on to the boats, then with long poles push from the shore out upon the bosom of the mighty river. No farewells are uttered, no words spoken. Each man knows his duty, and performs it energetically; for they are not hirelings, these men of stout hearts and muscular arms. Nor is it a light task to guide those unwieldy scows through drifting ice, across that mile-wide river.*13

FAR LEFT: *This fife and drum belonged to William Clayton and is now found in the Heber C. Kimball home.* LEFT: *A depiction of Luman Shurtliff bowing his head in prayer before leaving the Nauvoo Temple.* ABOVE: *A depiction of the Young family preparing to leave Nauvoo.*

$\mathcal{L}$ucius Scovil, who owned and ran a bakery in
Nauvoo, waited till May of 1846 to leave Nauvoo so
his pregnant wife could deliver her baby. She died
giving birth to twins, Mary and Martha. Ten days
later the twins died. On May sixth he received
a mission call to England. He traveled with his
remaining family a few days, made arrangements
for someone to care for them, then blessed them.
In England he commissioned 150 dozen temple
plates, which financed his and Heber C. Kimball's
mission. Lucius wrote:

> *This seemed like a painful duty for me to perform,*
> *to leave my family to go into the wilderness*
> *and I to turn and go the other way. It cost*
> *all that I had on this earth…[but] I thought*
> *it was best to round up my shoulders like a bold*
> *soldier of the crop…, and assist in rolling forth*
> *the Kingdom of God.*14

I was five years old when we started from Nauvoo. We crossed over the Mississippi in the skiff in the dusk of the evening. We bid goodbye to our dear old feeble grandmother, Lucy Mack Smith. I can never forget the bitter tears she shed when she bid us goodbye for the last time in this life. She knew it would be the last time she would see her son's family....15

—Martha Ann Smith, Hyrum and Mary Fielding's daughter

June 1, 1846, Sally Randall's letter explains:

We expect to start in a few days for the West. Where we shall go I know not, but we are going into the wilderness. We go as Abraham went, not knowing whither we go, but the Lord will go before us, and be our front and rearward. The Saints have been going steady since last February and are still going by hundreds. They cross the river in several places and cross day and night.... You think there is no need of going from here, but the mob are threatening continually to come upon us. We heard they were coming today but I have not seen anything in the least, for I believe there is faith enough in the city to keep them back until the Saints all get away.... Most of the Saints are selling out although at a very low price. I expect the temple will be sold. The Roman Catholics talk of buying it. 16

FAR LEFT: *As the Saints left Nauvoo, some fathers separated from their families and continued on missions. Taken at the end of Parley Street.* ABOVE LEFT: *A replica of the Nauvoo Temple plate that Scovil commissioned to pay for his mission.* LEFT: *Depiction of Lucy Mack Smith on the bank of the Mississippi saying good-bye to her granddaughter.*

"*I*f it was so hard to leave a city and a temple built with such labor and sacrifice, it must have been even more difficult to leave behind, probably never to be visited again, the final resting place of so many loved ones…. [T]here were few, if any, families taking one last look back across the Mississippi who were not thinking of dear ones left behind in the silent burial grounds of Nauvoo."17

Nauvoo was a healthy city with people of other religions living peacefully with the Saints. Joseph Smith greatly admired the Catholic priests in the area, who faithfully attended to their congregations and left the Latter-day Saints to worship and live as they saw fit.

All residents of Nauvoo became victims of the mob. Many residents volunteered to defend the city, including new non-LDS families, known as "the new citizens," who had bought out the Saints. Jacob B. Backenstos had been a representative in the legislature when the Nauvoo charter was repealed. He quit the legislature, ran for sheriff of Hancock County, and won. He was immediately pressured to leave but was not intimidated. Caught alone by the mob, he outdistanced them and deputized a group of men who defended the sheriff and killed Frank Worell, the person in charge of the Carthage Greys at the prison when Joseph and Hyrum were martyred.

A small, brave group of defenders of the city coalesced, called, "The Spartan Band." They did what they could until mobs overwhelmed the city, ending "The Battle of Nauvoo" with a negotiated peace, which didn't hold—finally leaving the city to anarchy. Benjamin Ashby wrote:

LEFT: Depiction of family saying good-bye to loved ones in the Pioneer Burial Grounds. The child death rate of Nauvoo was 64% for three reasons: malaria on the flats, inadequate housing and extra physical labor required to reestablish homes after the exile.[18]
ABOVE: This view of the Temple includes newly constructed houses in the foreground.

On the day of the Nauvoo Battle amidst the distant sound of rattling musketry and the boom of cannon, we took up the line of march for the distant camp on the Mississippi River. At night we could hear the sound of the bell and the bass drum from the tower of the temple where the mob were carousing after banishing from their pleasant homes, innocent men, women and children to perish in the wilderness.

We camped a week during which Father yielded up his life a martyr to the cause of truth and the gospel. Mother had a few dollars and I went back to a sawmill and purchased some oak boards sufficient to make him a coffin.... We buried him in a grove by the side of a little child of brother and sister Parmers.[19]

At the surrender of Nauvoo, the fugitive Saints were anxious to take with them whatever property they could. Nothing was as important as their rifles and ammunition. The mobbers demanded the arms and ammunition of all who left the city, and even searched their wagons to see none was taken.

Eunice McRae, wife of the leader of "The Spartan Band" (the last defenders of the city), was determined to save a keg of powder. She sat in the front of the wagon on a powder keg covered with her skirt. She drove the wagon alone, nine months pregnant, with five young sons ages two to thirteen years. A squad of the enemy came searching her wagon. She coolly asked, "How many times are you going to search this wagon?"[20] They sent her directly out of the city and she saved her powder.

We hurried to pack some food, cooking utensils, clothing and bedding, which was afterward unpacked and strewn over the ground by the mob as they searched for firearms. Mother had some bread already in the kettles to bake. Of course she did not have time to bake, so she hung it on the reach of our wagon and cooked it after we crossed the Mississippi River.[21]

—Mary Field Garner

ABOVE: *A depiction of Eunice McRae, hiding a barrel of gunpowder.* RIGHT: *A depiction of Saints bowed in prayer near the Seventies Hall as they prepare to leave Nauvoo.*

> *It seemed as though there was some-thing more than human nature which caused them to feel so joyful and happy to leave their comfortable homes and to go out in the dead of winter with so many young children, to face the cold and the storms, and not even knowing where they were going. It seemed to me that we must be in possession of some power besides the power of man.* 22
>
> —George Whitaker

ABOVE: *A daylight view of the temple from the Trail of Hope.* RIGHT: *Depiction of the Saints as they leave Nauvoo, past the Seventies Hall and down the Trail of Hope to the Mississippi.*

Come, come, ye Saints, no toil or labor fear; But with joy wend your way.
Though hard to you this journey may appear, grace shall be as your day.
'Tis better far for us to strive, our useless cares from us to drive;
Do this, and joy, your hearts will swell—All is well! All is well! 22

— William Clayton, April 1846, while camped at Locust Creek

ENDNOTES

TITLE PAGE

1. George D. Smith, ed., *An Intimate Chronicle: The Journals of William Clayton* (Salt Lake City: Signature Books, 1995), p. 252.

CHRONOLOGY

Church History in the Fulness of Times: The History of The Church of Jesus Christ of Latter-day Saints. Prepared by the Church Educational System. (Published by author. Salt Lake City, 1993); Drew S. Goodman, *The Fullness of Times: A Chronological Comparison of Important Events in Church, U.S., and World History* (Salt lake City: Eagle Gate, 2001); George Givens and Sylvia Givens, *Nauvoo Fact Book: Questions and Answers for Nauvoo Enthusiasts* (Lynchberg, Virginia: Parley Street Publishers, 2000).

BEGINNING AT COMMERCE

1. Susan Easton Black and Richard E. Bennett, eds., *A City of Refuge: Quincy, Illinois* (Salt Lake City: Millennial Press, 2000), p. 1.
2. Ibid., p. 73.
3. Orville Browning, quoted in *HC*, 4:370.
4. Joseph Smith, *History of the Church of Jesus Christ of Latter-day Saints*, 7 vols., ed. B. H. Roberts (Salt Lake City: Deseret Book, 1976). 3:375; **hereafter referred to as *HC*.**
5. Ibid.; see also Roberts, B. H., ed. *Comprehensive History of the Church*, Reprinted by Corporation of the President, The Church of Jesus Christ of Latter-day Saints, Provo, Utah: Brigham Young University Press, 1965, 2:9; **hereafter referred to as *CHC*.**
6. *HC*, 3:349.
7. *HC*, 4:3 ftn.; see also Orson F. Whitney, *Life of Heber C. Kimball* (Salt Lake City: Bookcraft, 1945), pp. 263–64.
8. Ibid.

BUILDING A "CITY BEAUTIFUL"

1. Stanley B. Kimball, "Nauvoo," *Improvement Era*, July 1962, p. 548; quoted in John Telford, *Nauvoo*, text by Susan Easton Back and Kim C. Averett (Salt Lake City: Deseret Book,

1997), p. 6.
2. Warren Foote, quoted in George W. Givens, *In Old Nauvoo: Everyday Life in the City of Joseph* (Salt Lake City: Deseret Book., 1990), p. 22.
3. Sally Randall Letters, Church Historical Department, LDS Church Archives; quoted in Givens, *In Old Nauvoo*, p. 82. See also Kenneth W. Godfrey, Audrey M. Godfrey, and Jill, Mulvay Derr, *Women's Voices: An Untold History of the Latter-day Saints*, 1830–1900 (Salt Lake City: Deseret Book, 1982), p. 135.
4. Richard Neitzel Holzapfel and Jeni Broberg Holzapfel, *Women of Nauvoo* (Salt Lake City: Bookcraft, 1992), p. 39.
5. Ibid.
6. E. Cecil McGavin, *Nauvoo, the Beautiful* (Salt Lake City: Stevens and Wallis, 1946), p. 256.
7. *HC*, 4:417.
8. *HC*, 4:608–609
9. Telford, *Nauvoo*, p. 33.
10. Givens, *In Old Nauvoo*, pp. 25, 97.
11. Ibid., p. 4.
12. Ibid., p. 5.
13. Givens and Givens, *Nauvoo Fact Book*, p. 135.
14. Ibid., p.169.
15. Ibid., pp. 100, 169.
16. Givens, *In Old Nauvoo*, p. 74.
17. Ibid., p. 68.
18. Ibid., p. 73.
19. Dale Berge, "The Jonathan Browning Site: An Example of Archaeology for Restoration in Nauvoo, Illinois," *BYU Studies*, 19 (2) Winter 1979, p. 206.
20. Ibid.
21. Ibid.
22. Givens, *In Old Nauvoo*, p. 265.
23. *HC*, 6:185.
24. Givens, *In Old Nauvoo*, pp. 207–208.
25. Ibid., p. 198.
26. *HC*, 5:367.
27. Givens, *In Old Nauvoo*, p. 266.
28. Ibid., p. 203.
29. David R. Crockett, *Saints in Exile: A Day by Day Pioneer Experience, Nauvoo to Council Bluffs* (Tucson, Arizona: LDS-Gems Press, 1996), p. 363.
30. *Nauvoo Fact Book*, p. 1; Telford, Black, *Nauvoo*, p. 38.
31. Givens, *In Old Nauvoo*, p. 200.

32. Ibid.
33. Givens, *In Old Nauvoo*, p. 7.

SUSTAINING A FAMILY

1. Sarah D. Rich Autobiography, LDS Church Archives; quoted in Richard Neitzel Holzapfel and Jeni Broberg Holzapfel, *Women of Nauvoo* (Salt Lake City: Bookcraft, 1992), p. 47.
2. George W. Givens, *In Old Nauvoo: Everyday Life in the City of Joseph* (Salt Lake City: Deseret Book, 1990), p. 187.
3. Ibid., p. 217.
4. Ibid., p. 190.
5. Ibid., p. 218.
6. Richard Jackson, "The Mormon Village," *BYU Studies*, Winter 1977; quoted in Givens, *In Old Nauvoo*, p. 237.
7. Givens, *In Old Nauvoo*, p. 246.
8. Ibid., p. 230.
9. Ibid., p. 231.
10. Ibid., p. 246.
11. Ibid., pp. 249–50.
12. Daniel H. Ludlow, *Church History: Selections from the Encyclopedia of Mormonism* (Salt Lake City: Deseret Book, 1992), p. 368.
13. "The Seventies Hall at Nauvoo," published by Nauvoo Restoration, Inc.
14. *Journal of Discourses,* **hereafter referred to as *JD*,** 6:150.

PREPARING A PEOPLE

1. William G. Hartley, "The Knight Family: Ever Faithful to the Prophet," *Ensign*, Jan 1989, p. 43.
2. Ibid.
3. Ibid.
4. Vicky Burgess-Olson, *Sister Saints* (Provo, Utah: Brigham Young University Press, 1978), p. 204.
5. Edward W. Tullidge, *Women of Mormondom* (New York: Tullidge and Crandall, 1877). Reprinted Salt Lake City, 1975.
6. Bathsheba W. Smith; quoted in Richard Neitzel Holzapfel and Jeni Broberg Holzapfel, *Women of Nauvoo* (Salt Lake City: Bookcraft, 1992), p. 51.
7. Ibid.
8. Richard Neitzel Holzapfel, and T. Jeffery Cottle, *Old Mormon Nauvoo and Southeastern Iowa: Historic

Photographs and Guide* (Santa Ana, California: Fieldbrook Productions, 1991), pp. 77–78.
9. Emerson Roy West, *Profiles of the Presidents* (Salt Lake City: Deseret Book, 1980), p. 111.
10. Wilford Woodruff, quoted in *Church History in the Fulness of Times: The History of The Church of Jesus Christ of Latter-day Saints*. Prepared by the Church Educational System. (Published by author. Salt Lake City, 1993), p. 227.
11. Daniel H. Ludlow, *Church History: Selections from the Encyclopedia of Mormonism* (Salt Lake City: Deseret Book, 1992), p. 631.
12. Matthias F. Cowley, *Wilford Woodruff: History of His Life and Labors* (Salt Lake City: Bookcraft, 1964), pp. 476–77.
13. Orson F. Whitney, *Life of Heber C. Kimball* (Salt Lake City: Bookcraft, 1945), p. 313.
14. Ibid.
15. Stanley B. Kimball, ed., *On the Potter's Wheel: The Diaries of Heber C. Kimball* (Salt Lake City: Signature Books, 1987), p. 53.
16. Vilate Kimball, quoted in Holzapfel and Holzapfel, *Women of Nauvoo*, p. 50.
17. *JD*, 4:222.
18. *HC*, 7:466.
19. *JD*, 8:173.
20. Leonard J. Arrington, *Brigham Young: American Moses* (Urbana and Chicago: University of Illinois Press, 1986), p. 86.
21. Emmeline B. Wells, "Biography of Mary Ann Angell Young" *The Juvenile Instructor* 26 (1 Jan. 1891), pp. 56–57; quoted in Arrington, *Brigham Young: American Moses*, p. 86.
22. Dean C. Jessee, "Brigham Young's Family, Part I, 1824–45," *BYU Studies*, 18 (no. 3) Spring 1978, p. 319.
23. Ibid.
24. Ibid.
25. George W. Givens, *In Old Nauvoo: Everyday Life in the City of Joseph* (Salt Lake City: Deseret Book, 1990), p. 9.
26. Brigham Young Journal, May 31, 1843; reprinted by Nauvoo Restoration Inc.
27. Richard L. Jensen, "The John Taylor Family," *Ensign*, Feb. 1980, pp. 50–56.

28. Ibid.
29. Ibid.
30. Whitney, *Life of Heber C. Kimball*, p. 144.
31. Willard Richards Journals, LDS Church Archives, Salt Lake City, Utah; quoted in *Old Mormon Nauvoo*, p. 76.
32. *Journal History of The Church of Jesus Christ of Latter-day Saints*, Church Historical Department, Salt Lake City, Utah, 21 November 1841.
33. *HC*, 6:619.
34. *HC*, 6:616.
35. *Old Mormon Nauvoo*, p. 76.
36. Hoyt W. Brewster, Jr., *Doctrine and Covenants Encyclopedia* (Salt Lake City: Bookcraft, 1988), p. 528; quoted in Russell M. Ballard, "Legacy of Hyrum," *Ensign*, Sept. 1994, p. 56.
37. *Conference Report*, Oct. 1920, p. 89; quoted in Ballard, "Legacy of Hyrum," pp. 57.
38. Doctrine and Covenants, 124:15.
39. Lucy Mack Smith. *History of the Prophet Joseph Smith*, p. 55.
40. Doctrine and Covenants, 124:95.
41. *HC*, 2:338.
42. Holzapfel and Holzapfel, *Women of Nauvoo*, p. 73.
43. Joseph Fielding Smith, quoted in M. Russell Ballard, "Brothers Bound by Love and Faith," *Ensign*, Sept. 1994, p. 65.

REJOICING WITH A PROPHET

1. Richard Neitzel Holzapfel and T. Jeffery Cottle, *Old Mormon Nauvoo…* (Santa Ana, California: Fieldbrook Productions, 1991), pp. 11–12.
2. *HC*, 6:133.
3. Lucy Mack Smith, *History of the Joseph Smith by His Mother*, Preston Nibley, ed. (Salt Lake City: Bookcraft, 1958), pp. 190–91.
4. *HC*, 6:165–66.
5. Richard Neitzel Holzapfel and Jeni Broberg Holzapfel, *Women of Nauvoo* (Salt Lake City: Bookcraft, 1992), p. 20.
6. Cannon, *Life of Joseph Smith*, p. 20.
7. Lucy Mack Smith, quoted in Janet Peterson and LaRene Gaunt, *Elect Ladies: Presidents of the Relief Society* (Salt Lake City: Deseret Book, 1990), p. 12.

8. Emmeline B. Wells, quoted in Holzapfel and Holzapfel, *Women of Nauvoo*, p. 156.
9. John A. Widstoe, *Joseph Smith: Seeker After Truth, Prophet of God* (Salt Lake City: Bookcraft, 1957), p. 351.
10. Scot Facer Proctor, *Witness of the Light: A Photographic Journey in the Footsteps of the American Prophet Joseph Smith* (Salt Lake City, Deseret Book, 1991), p. 203.
11. Widstoe, *Joseph Smith*, pp. 350–351.
12. Lavina Fielding Anderson, "They Came to Nauvoo," *Ensign*, Sept. 1979, p. 21.
13. Ibid.
14. George Givens and Sylvia Givens, *Nauvoo Fact Book: Questions and Answers for Nauvoo Enthusiasts* (Lynchberg, Virginia: Parley Street Publishers, 2000), p. 92.
15. E. Cecil McGavin, *Nauvoo, the Beautiful* (Salt Lake City: Stevens and Wallis, 1946), p. 80.
16. Ibid.
17. Hyrum L. Andrus and Helen Mae Andrus, *They Knew the Prophet* (Salt Lake City: Bookcraft, 1974), p. 127.
18. *In Old Nauvoo*, p. 147.
19. Ibid., pp. 147–48.
20. Ibid.
21. *JD*, 5:332.
22. *JD*, 3:51.
23. Widstoe, *Joseph Smith*, p. 276.
24. Ibid., pp. 352–53.
25. Ibid., p. 352.
26. Leonard J. Arrington, *Brigham Young: American Moses* (Urbana and Chicago: University of Illinois Press, 1986), p. 60.
27. Janet Peterson and LaRene Gaunt, *Elect Ladies: Presidents of the Relief Society* (Salt Lake City: Deseret Book, 1990), p. 15–16.
28. Ibid, p. 19.
29. *JD*, 4:297.

LOSING A BELOVED PROPHET
1. *HC*, 1:30.
2. E. Cecil McGavin, *Nauvoo, the Beautiful* (Salt Lake City: Stevens and Wallis, 1946), p. 150.
3. Richard Neitzel Holzapfel, Alexander L. Baugh, Robert C. Freeman, and Andrew H. Hedges, *On This Day in the Church: An Illustrated Almanac of the Latter-day Saints* (Salt Lake City: Eagle Gate), 2000, p. 56.
4. Smith, Joseph Fielding, *Essentials in Church History* (The Church of Jesus Christ of Latter-day Saints: Salt Lake City, 1922), pp. 298–99.
5. Ibid., p. 365.
6. Ibid., p. 366.
7. *HC*, 6:408.
8. Ibid, 6:545.
9. Ibid., 6:546.
10. Ibid., 6:551; see also *CHC*, 2:246–47.
11. *CHC*, 2:250.
12. *HC*, 6:500.
13. David B. Haight, "Joseph Smith, the Prophet, *Ensign*, Dec. 2001, pp. 32–33.
14. Benjamin Ashby Autobiography, BYU Special Collections, Provo, Utah, p. 3.
15. Haight, "Joseph Smith, the Prophet," *Ensign*, p. 33.
16. *HC*, 5:498.
17. Lavina Fielding Anderson, "They Came to Nauvoo," *Ensign*, Sept. 1979, p. 21.
18. D&C 135:3.
19. *HC*, 6:500; Haight, "Joseph Smith, the Prophet," *Ensign*, p. 30.
20. M. Russell Ballard, "Brothers Bound by Love and Faith," Ensign, Sept. 1994, p. 64.
21. Ibid.
22. Ibid.
23. *HC*, 4:461.

Stan Watts, craftsman for the new Nauvoo Temple

FINISHING A TEMPLE
1. *Luman Shurtliff Autobiography*, quoted in John Telford, *Nauvoo*, text by Susan Easton Back and Kim C. Averett (Salt Lake City: Deseret Book, 1997), p. 57.
2. George W. Givens, *In Old Nauvoo: Everyday Life in the City of Joseph* (Salt Lake City: Deseret Book, 1990), p. 234.
3. Ibid., pp. 20–21.
4. Richard O. Cowan, "Nauvoo Temple," in Susan Easton Black and Richard E. Bennett, eds., *A City of Refuge: Quincy, Illinois* (Salt Lake City: Millennial Press, 2000), p. 283.
5. Janet Peterson and LaRene Gaunt, *Elect Ladies: Presidents of the Relief Society* (Salt Lake City: Deseret Book, 1990), p. 1.
6. *Church History in the Fulness of Times: The History of The Church of Jesus Christ of Latter-day Saints*. Prepared by the Church Educational System. Published by author. Salt Lake City, 1993, p. 249.
7. Record of the Female Relief Society of Nauvoo, 26 Mar. 1842, LDS Church Archives, pp. 18–19; quoted in Janath Cannon, *Nauvoo Panorama* (Nauvoo Restoration, Inc., 1991), p. 1.
8. Wandle Mace Autobiography, quoted in Telford, *Nauvoo*, p. 62.
9. B. H. Roberts, *Outlines of Ecclesiastical History*, 3rd ed. (Salt Lake City: Deseret News, 1902), p. 394.
10. Wandle Mace Autobiography, quoted in Telford, *Nauvoo*, p. 62.
11. Peterson and Gaunt, *Elect Ladies*, p. 1.
12. Charles Lambert, quoted in Maurine Jensen Proctor, and Scot Facer Proctor, *The Gathering: Mormon Pioneers on the Trail to Zion* (Salt Lake City: Deseret Book, 2000), pp. 53–54.
13. M. Russell Ballard, "The Legacy of Hyrum." *Ensign*, Sept. 1994, p. 57; see also *HC*, 6:298.
14. Lavina Fielding Anderson, "They Came to Nauvoo," *Ensign*, Sept. 1979, p. 21.
15. Telford, *Nauvoo*, p. 58; see also *HC*, 5:58.
16. R. Scott Lloyd, "Crafting, Shaping Prepared Him for Sublime Task," *Church News*, 3 Feb. 2001.
17. J. Earl Arrington, "William Weeks, Architect of the Nauvoo Temple," BYU Studies 9 (Spring 1979), p. 343; quoted in Telford, *Nauvoo*, p. 57.
18. Joseph Fielding, quoted in Givens, *In Old Nauvoo*, p. 6.
19. Cowan, "Nauvoo Temple," in Black and Bennett, *A City of Refuge*, p. 284.
20. Ibid., 285
21. Cowley, Matthias F., *Wilford Woodruff: History of His Life and Labors* (Salt Lake City: Bookcraft, 1964), p. 158; see also Cowan, "Nauvoo Temple," in Black and Bennett, *A City of Refuge*, p. 286.
22. Matthew B. Brown and Paul Thomas Smith, *Symbols in Stone: Symbolism on the Early Temples of the Restoration* (American Fork, Utah: Covenant Communications, 1997), p. 105.
23. Cowan, "Nauvoo Temple,"in Black and Bennett, *A City of Refuge*, p. 275.
24. Moses 7:53.
25. Journal of Wandle Mace, quoted in Matthew B. Brown, *The Gate of Heaven: Insights on the Doctrines and Symbols of the Temple* (American Fork, Utah: Covenant Communications, 1999), p. 220.
26. Brown, *The Gate of Heaven*, p. 220.
27. Gordon B. Hinckley, "This Peaceful House of God," *Ensign*, May 1993, p. 27.
28. *Church News*, Oct 30, 1999, p. 7.
29. Gordon B. Hinckley, "Thanks to the Lord for His Blessings," *Ensign*, May 1999, p. 89.

Gino Vail, craftsman for the new Nauvoo Temple

LEAVING THE "CITY BEAUTIFUL"
1. *HC*, 6:222.
2. Ibid., 6:377.
3. David R. Crockett, *Saints in Exile: A Day by Day Pioneer Experience, Nauvoo to Council Bluffs* (Tucson, Arizona: LDS-Gems Press, 1996), p. 1.
4. Ibid., p. 2.
5. Bathsheba W. Smith, quoted in Richard Neitzel Holzapfel and Jeni Broberg Holzapfel, *Women of Nauvoo* (Salt Lake City: Bookcraft, 1992), p. 142.
6. Margaret Judd Clawson, inscribed on Trail of Hope Marker on Parley Street.
7. Crockett, *Saints in Exile*, p. 132.
8. Bathsheba W. Smith, inscribed on Trail of Hope Marker, Parley Street.
9. Peter Conover, quoted in Crockett, *Saints in Exile*, p. 62.
10. Richard Neitzel Holzapfel and T. Jeffery Cottle, *Old Mormon Nauvoo and Southeastern Iowa: Historic Photographs and Guide* (Santa Ana, California: Fieldbrook Productions, 1991), p.89.
11. Luman Shurtliff, Autobiography, quoted in Crockett, *Saints in Exile*, p. 303.
12. Ibid., p. 169.
13. John R. Young, quoted in Crockett, *Saints in Exile*, p. 149.
14. Wilford Woodruff Journals, Feb. 8, 1857, LDS Church Archives, Salt Lake City, Utah; quoted in Maurine Jensen Proctor, and Scot Facer Proctor, *The Gathering: Mormon Pioneers on the Trail to Zion* (Salt Lake City: Deseret Book, 2000), p. 34.
15. Martha Ann Smith, inscribed on Trail of Hope Marker, Parley Street; quoted in Don Cecil Corbett, *Mary Fielding Smith, Daughter of Britain* (Salt Lake City: Deseret Book, 1970), p. 195.
16. Crockett, *Saints in Exile*, p. 346.
17. George W. Givens, *In Old Nauvoo: City of Joseph* (Salt Lake City: Deseret Book, 1990), p. 113.
18. Ibid., p. 113–114.
19. Benjamin Ashby Autobiography, BYU Special Collections, Provo, Utah.
20. Edward W. Tullidge, *Women of Mormondom* (New York: Tullidge and Crandall, 1877), pp. 425–26.
21. Mary Field Garner, quoted on Trail of Hope Marker, Parley Street.
22. George Whitaker, "Life of George Whitaker, a Utah Pioneer, 1820–1907," Typescript, p. 12, Church Archives.
23. *Hymns of The Church of Jesus Christ of Latter-day Saints*, (Salt Lake City: The Church of Jesus Christ of Latter-day Saints, 1985), no. 30.

INDEX